Concise 'Reality Harmonizing' Quotes
From
Reality Harmonizer Bob

Love Truth Over Misconception

I do not discriminate against writing a periodic enlightening, comical quote in this book, although there are very few. I do believe that many concepts I find are of high value, because that is what I search hard for. I no doubt have a unique positive energy in being intensely and endlessly observant in search of what is more important and helpful in life versus what is vain, distracts us from true peace, and what is more important versus things that cause us to have misconceptions aside from popular, greedy, and intentional lies.

I worked to recognize influential concepts and to jot them down in short and concise sentences in this book, but if I feel a need to explain a quote then I will put some explanation below my quote.

"Harmonize the reality of what you can and cannot see with God's truth, Spirit and Biblical guidance." Reality Harmonizer Bob

SECTION 1:

1) God loves you too, not just me.

Explanation: My first experience in being drawn to God-Christ's-Spirit by hearing the story about His power of life and love in healing a blind man caused me to desire and trust in Christ as Lord of Heaven and Earth, which represents both the future and the now, and I was confident that He is so accommodating of peace and joy that I wanted Him ALL FOR MYSELF as I viewed many people in this World as unhappy. I knew God loved me and I accepted it; I did not care what anyone else thought about it. I did not want unhappy people interfering with my joy; however, I did want people to experience the same lasting joy from Christ.

I started to leave this quote without explanation, because I wanted some to view it as a funny, sarcastic arrogant like statement for the sake of it catching the mind and attention in more than one way; however, I did not want some to qualify looking at it as a truly arrogant statement. I am no more especially Human than anyone else, except that I have chosen God's peace and I exercise faith in God's peace as anyone else can.

God loves us all and He gives us the exact same invitation of Heaven and Earth with Him as our Lord, and I hope to be a part of trying to relay that message with attempted clarity to as many people as possible, ideally to everyone. God loves you too, not just me; I simply experience it, because I accept it via resurrected Christ's evidence and eternally reconciling invite despite our Human failures and weaknesses.

2) I search my brain for obvious things we commonly overlook.

3) Acknowledging one race from God acknowledges human equality.

4) Faith lasts as long as its source.

5) Anyone who succeeds at being born should oppose abortion.

6) A womb is not a tomb it is a human child's first room.

7) Dead gods = Dead religions = False religions.

8) Support children having their parents by supporting natural marriage.

9) When lies become our laws then flies become our Pa's.

10) Evolution declares the racism of unequal evolved races from animals.

11) Biblical Creation reveals one human race from God, Adam, and Eve.

12) One race is proven by all coming from Noah's family after the worldwide flood.

13) Jesus is as real as life and death.

14) Everyone faces death, but Christ rose from the dead and never died again via the supreme power as one with God the Father.

15) The Bible is a preeminent History book revealing only one human race.

16) The Bible is not just a History book, but is God speaking through many generations.

17) The command to "love neighbors" does not exist without Christ and His Bible.

18) God created the World with words.

19) Create eternal hope and love using God's Spirit and truth words in faith.

20) Hate war, but hate the slavery of violent assaults and lies more.

21) Keeping God's neighborly "law and order" helps to prevent wars.

22) God's ten commandments gives everyone property rights and the right to life.

23) Love people with Christ's forgiveness, Spirit fruit, and eternal truth.

24) We cannot steal one day from God, and we lose out trying to.

25) Real hope begins where vain worldly hope ends.

26) Caffeine is a mind, adrenaline, and nerve altering drug.

27) Coffee is a dehydrating laxative and diuretic.

28) There is more work to do on our mind than on the whole earth.

29) Gluttony does not love us back.

30) Many people still don't know Democrat Americans fought a war to keep slavery.

31) Many people still don't know Republican Americans fought a war to end slavery.

32) God's love is for everyone as revealed by His forgiveness on the cross.

33) God's cross forgiveness is real because of His resurrection power.

34) God showed us the power of Heaven when Christ ascended from the Earth.

35) Speaking about Christ's resurrected Lordship values your life and your neighbor's lives.

36) Believing in God's Trinitarian resurrection power saves you. (Romans 10:9)

37) Real hope is confidence in the 2nd life by trusting resurrected Christ as Lord.

38) Christian safety nets make more sense than negative "Christian accountability" groups.

39) Do not fear being on God's side - fear being against Him.

40) God does not promise tomorrow and the next life is too late to choose Him.

41) Why like pain instead of liking peace and comfort which Heaven's God represents.

42) What is wrong with peace and comfort? Desire it under God in its real form.

43) Do not trust a dead opossum.

44) I want a better World, a better appetite, better energy and better communion.

45) What makes someone not want a more peaceful World in this life and the next?

46) Don't you want a better World with God-Christ's-Spirit of Comfort?

47) I have trusted the best comforting Holy Spirit that lasts eternally from Christ.

48) Repentance is not a shame or burden - it is a gift to choose.

49) Don't let your mind steal inner peace - renew its focus daily on the infinite.

50) Take lessons from true hope that never dies, because its source in Christ never dies.

51) There is no more pregnancy or abortion in Christ's Heaven.

52) Real racists oppose "one nation under God."

53) Maybe 'love is patient and kind' because it is not an emotion. (1 Corinthians 13)

54) Love 'always hopes', which improves emotions, but is faith linked not an emotion.

55) Lasting love initiates duty of compassion, because it comes from sovereign love.

56) Christian prayer is faith that you truly are not alone and perfect peace is there for you.

57) For economic success we have commit to our work despite periodic claustrophobia.

58) Jobs can sometimes feel like slavery or prison but they aren't = work is a necessity.

59) Exercising Christian principles initiates working with hope, purpose and peace of heart.

60) Spiritual humility recognizes our limits while pursuing contentment without pessimism.

61) If you rarely meet imperfect people under God, enjoy more alone time with God.

62) What good do I know that you can't know? Nothing, God grants wisdom to His seekers.

63) If forgiveness did not exist neither would people.

64) Forgiveness is the path where wisdom can walk.

65) Forgiveness is neither a decision for or against pardon; it allows neighborly justice.
66) God gives you a 2nd chance everyday; in safe situations give others the same.

67) We need to impress a potential employer as peaceable and safe versus staying angry.

68) Think according to one day at a time, because that is all we have, if that much.

69) Plan to live 120 years, and also realize any day could be your last.

70) Be optimistic for Christ's Heaven, and enjoy your time in loving creation from God.

71) When your body does not cooperate - thank God for Heaven.

72) When your mind fails - remember 1 thing = your mind will work in Christ's Heaven.

73) When you love patience but can't find it - drink needed water and assess need.

74) Do not hate God's peace.

75) Do not hate Police - Police yourself rightly, and view Police as backup.

76) Democrat media lies about self-defense cases to promote illegitimate revenge violence.

77) Why pretend violent thieves are victims of those they assaulted? Democrat media is a thief.

78) Unrepentant thieves are a problem NOT repentant thieves.

79) The most active unrepentant thief is lying Democrat media getting bystanders killed.

80) Psychological warfare by media lying for violent revenge on innocence is major crime.

81) Prisons should be humane under God.

82) Prisons should be designed to teach people to be more peaceable before release.

83) Prisons should be for keeping the unrepentant violent until they prove

otherwise.

84) Prisons should find ways for thieves to reconcile & pay their debt while detained.

85) Prisons & Prisoners should equally be "Ten Commandment" protected under God as all people.

86) Society needs people to come out of Prison more peaceful than they went in.

87) Prisons should have helpful reconciling facilities detainment is enough punishment.

88) Prisons should be built to consider all safety and efficiency for everyone.

89) 2020's Democrat mobs showed the World that Humane Prisons can keep society safer.

90) Making Home ownership more attainable should decrease the Prison population.

91) People who do violence against Police belong in Prison.

92) Society needs to love and respect its Police.

93) Police should be respected and understood more while courts and sentencing standards should be more broadly questioned and assessed (discerned) more fairly.

94) A peaceful, educated society should know that Police simply escort suspects to talk about peacemaking and reconciliation.

95) Our justice & detaining system should be about discussions of peace & reconciliation.

96) "Love your neighbor" & the "Golden Rule" should be posted in jails, courts & Police venues.

97) Probably, no cult books or fiction should be allowed in reconciling jails – Fundamental Bible based books, and original translations of the Bible only. (King James Version, Hollman, Wycliffe, and versions closed

checked to be in accordance with those versions + original Greek and Hebrew texts…)

98) How can a prisoner train their mind rightly by studying fiction in detainment? Nobody can.

99) Prisoners should be treated with dignity & Prisoners should treat others with dignity.

100) It is not possible to grant full dignity to someone who is trying to bully you.

101) People cannot live rationally around others without forgiveness, patience & temperance.

102) Private property rights should be among the highest values in politics & governing.

103) If you cannot 'love your enemy', you cannot love yourself = We are our own most frequent enemy.

104) The way to understand these things is to have true faith in human equality from God.

105) Today's athletes are political slaves to Democrat media.

106) Democrats don't care about one person who cares about God's values.

107) How can Democrats care about Black people if they don't care about any person as Human from God versus an evolutionary animal?

108) Today's Democrats care about dividing people with violent loyalist groups for corrupt power.

109) Violent Democrat loyalist groups are against people having a pondered view point.

110) Violent Democrat loyalist groups are against "Freedom of Speech".

111) Violent Democrat loyalist groups are against people hearing both sides of a story.

112) Violent Democrat loyalist groups only want power, which hates truth & reality for people.

113) Proper perspective enjoys shopping for appropriate needs versus dreading it.

114) Proper perspective encourages efficiency needs stocking versus opposing administering grace + sowing and reaping for oneself.

115) Administering sowing and reaping grace to self for needs should be an obvious right.

116) We need Bibles in Prisons to counter Democrats from using Prisons to violently radicalize.

117) There should be ways to stop various supremacist groups from forming in Prisons.

118) There should be ways to stop Islamic radical groups from forming in Prisons.

119) There should be ways to stop Black and White racist groups from forming in Prisons.

120) The way to diminish Prison hate groups is to declare Biblical Human equality from God, Adam and Eve.

121) We should declare Biblical Human equality from God, Adam and Eve as our nation's stance, and that stance is in America's "Declaration Of Independence."

121) Proper equality acknowledges that we all need to exercise temperance & repentance...

122) Proper equality is clear = We all need to know that God means "love neighbors."

123) Proper equality is clear = We all need to understand universal reconciliation principles.

124) Proper equality is clear = We all need to recognize that no one is perfect.

125) Peace is not a competition.

126) Basic peace is quite simple = It simply asks people not to steal or assault.

127) Life should not be hard if people simply follow 2 rules = Don't steal + Don't assault.

128) Society simply cracking down against stealing & assault enormously improves living.

129) Societal knowledge need = knowing that stealing & harming people are the main things Police should protect and enforce against.

130) Competition is for fun, fitness & self-defense fitness. Peacemaking > competition.

131) Survival & successful living settings should not be competitive about settling disputes.

132) There are multiple reasons that peacemaking is the best lifestyle.

133) True peacemaking teaches and expects peacemaking from enemies of peace also.

134) True peacemaking oftentimes needs to enforce peacemaking but prefers diplomacy.

135) Peacemaking is lived via Christ's reconciliation principles, truth & Spirit fruit.

136) Republicans refusing Democrat slavery in the 1800's and still today in refusing complete Socialism - shows Republican sincerity in outlawing slavery.

137) No, America does not need to be slaves to Black racist groups who want legal slavery.

138) No matter how Black Democrats 'feel' or believe - legal slavery does NOT need to come back.

139) If one is crazy enough to assault the Police - they are likely the neighborhood bully.

140) Improved Prison systems are a must to keep Police assaulters off the streets.

141) Police are our property & peace protecting backup; a criminal hates peace & Police.

142) Police also need to have a better understanding of their purpose via God's laws.

143) Police surprisingly do a very good job despite groups removing God's laws.

144) Our Police & Courts need to have respect for God's 10 neighbor loving commands.

145) Our Prison keepers need to have respect for God's 10 neighbor loving commands.

146) God's ten neighbor & God loving commands need to be posted on all governing venues.

147) God bless and rise with.

148) "Planet MySkull" is me referencing my brain within my skull.

149) God-Christ's-Spirit matters more.

150) A boring World would be Tyrants having only one Global nation with no philosophy allowed.

151) Humans operating under pride are nonsensical.

152) I love peace, quiet and noise - peace is the common denominator.

153) Don't you want a better World where death is no longer an issue?

154) Don't you want a better World where there are no more lies?

155) Don't you want a better World where there is not more pain?

156) Don't you want a better World where there is no more sorrow?

157) Don't you want a better World where there is no more stress?

158) Living with Christ's Spirit gives hope in this World, and promises a painless Heaven.

159) Republican systems creating pay for labor is the opposite of racism and slavery.

160) How can anyone be against racism and then promote Evolution? They can't.

161) If anyone does not know what true racism is - how do they contest it?

162) No one is against murder who kills human fetus.

163) No one is against murder who supports killing a baby on their day of birth.

164) Many Democrat leaders now support killing a baby on their birthday.

165) I make many points to counter the Historic number of lies via media in modern times.

166) Modern Islamic slave regimes are protected from scrutiny by American Democrats.

167) The Bible eludes that sin and lies are slave masters - Democrat cracker mobs prove it.

168) Shame is most often a form of sinful pride.

169) People don't choose shallow memory, but they do choose a shallow heart & mind.

170) American Democrats are not diverse enough to accept an innocent baby.

171) The psychology of the mind is vast.

172) Tragedy often happens to people due to someone else's sin and not their own.

173) Democrats facilitating illegal slavery is not repentance from legal slavery.

174) Democrats trying to bring socialistic legal slavery is not repentance from slavery.

175) Hell is not a dirty subject - it is a place of dread to warn against.

176) Make your time have everlasting value.

177) Do not steal valuable time away from yourself.

178) Sometimes, I say something irrelevant, but that is a risk I take in researching.

179) Wear shoes in Public restrooms.

180) A top goal of this book is to give much good advice.

181) Rinse the plunger with disinfectant spray and an extra flush.

182) Why do Democrats disrespect LEGAL immigrants?

183) I suspect Democrats had European KKK (Antifa?) crossing our border illegally.

184) Turning down Heaven in favor of Hell makes no sense.

185) Do many Democrat voters really know what they are supporting?

186) Democrat leaders even brought problems into restrooms.

187) Democrat leaders had men with wigs taking over women's sports.

188) Democrats vote against the knowledge of one human race from God.

189) Keep a careful, watchful eye, not a condemning eye.

190) Real love exists - Democrat media just blocks hearing about it.

191) Nation building is far better than cramming all nations into one small one.

192) Nation building is far better than Democrats tearing down nations.

193) Natural marriage law is proper population control.

194) There will be no free nation to escape to under Democrat Global supremacy plan.

195) Democrats teach people to view the USA as a slave nation, but we are free.

196) USA has rightly been known as the King of freedom Worldwide.

197) Communism, Socialism, Marxism & Anarchy brings slavery back.

198) President Trump is the first "America First" President.

199) Our rights come from God not from Abortionists.

200) Human rights come from God not from Abortionists.

SECTION 2:

201) It is best for rights to come from God not from murderers.

202) Mothers are not always right = Abortion...

203) Democrats have predatory compassion not true compassion.

204) God matters more than life, because there is not life without Him.

205) God matters more than any generation that has ever lived.

206) I support Black-lives-matter to Jesus NOT to Democrat slave masters!

207) Thank God that Eve did not abort her children.

208) Time is NOT short = only earth time is short.

209) Hell's warnings are not crazy in my view = I run out of time to write each day; life is short.

210) The evidence of God is the most fulfilling investigation in existence.

211) Be overshadowed with understanding's desire.

212) Time is always urgent for promoting Heaven over Hell.

213) Do not let earthly ideals become illusions that ignore Hell.

214) When you are at a "Drive-In" & forget where you parked your car - check yourself!

215) Enjoy intellectual freedom daily and tune into truth & God's Spirit.

216) Democrats define Black & White people wrongly just like marriage & parenthood.

217) Black and White people are equally human created in God's image.

218) People do not have to act the way Democrats say they do.

219) Think of how many White Democrats support abortion just to kill Black babies.

220) Think of how many Black Democrats support abortion just to kill White babies.

221) Think of how many Democrats support abortion just to kill male babies.

222) Think of how many Democrats support abortion just to kill female babies.

223) Think of how many Democrats support abortion just to kill American babies.

224) Think of how many Democrats support abortion to harvest body parts.

225) Think of how many Democrats support abortion in favor of street pimping.

226) Think of how many Democrats support abortion in opposition to natural family.

227) Think of how many Democrats support abortion as population control extremists.

228) Think of how many Democrats support abortion in favor of international hate groups.

229) You do not need anyone's validation to share Christ's salvation.

230) Bad politics reign when people do not speak up for good.

231) Illegal gun smuggling is part of Democrats open border scheme.

232) Politics matter because there are good & bad politics, support good.

233) Politics matter because we get to choose positive leaders vs negative.

234) Politics matter because we need good laws not bad ones.

235) Politics matter because God created politics.

236) Politics matter because we need order not mob rule.

237) Politics matter because we need to promote reverence for God.

238) Politics matter because evil tyrants want to take over.

239) Politics matter so that lives can matter instead of just a Dictator.

240) The DRA is the 'Democrat Rifle Association' that smuggled at the border.

241) Is the DRA diminishing now with the wall being built? Likely.

242) Are there more living unrepentant murderers in American than babies?

243) Democrats have created a society against death penalty for murderers.

244) Democrats have created a society that gives innocent babies the death penalty.

245) White Democrats are racist & there is a White American drug cartel.

246) The truth is humble.

247) Opposing freedom lovers by calling them racist is opposing freedom not racism!

248) Opposing Christ lovers by calling them racist opposes Christ not racism!

249) Opposing free market lovers by calling them racist opposes free markets not racism!

250) Opposing Police by calling them racist opposes people property protection not racism!

251) Opposing Police by calling them racist is supporting thieves not opposing racism!

252) Opposing Police by calling them racist supports neighborhood bullies not opposing racism!

253) Some pretend to be dumb but are inconsiderate, spiteful and/or oppressive.

254) Dumbness is usually the choice refusal to exercise sense.

255) Focus on tomorrow over yesterday and today over both.

256) If God could rise from the dead - would you believe in Him then?

257) Be wise enough to stand up for God's neighborly commandments.

258) Democrats supported true racist extremists crossing the borders illegally.

259) Heaven's peace is 100% all the time.

260) The good news is that it's ultimately about Christ's testimony not ours.

261) Christ's testimony in me is faith, hope, love & believing His redemption.

262) I am regularly redeemed to Christ for Christ, me & other believers despite naysayers.

263) True believers know they need Christ's redemption for life permanently.

264) True believers know they need Christ's redemption regularly for purification.

265) True believers know all need purification regularly no matter how big or small the sin.

266) True believers know that waking to a new day and not valuing Christ is a sin.

267) True believers know that not valuing people's eternal choice awareness is a sin.

268) True believers know that not 'walking in the Spirit' is a sin.

269) True believers know that all Christians wrestle with vain temptations.

270) True believers know that God forgives, or else people could not go on living.

271) True believers know that God's forgiveness opens communion in His goodness.

272) True believers know that forgiveness works and unforgiveness is wasteful.

273) Our testimony of faith in Christ matters far more than our accomplishments or rap sheets.

274) Your testimony of faith, hope and love in Christ for eternity matters most.

275) It is an extreme danger for those who do not have a testimony of faith in Christ for eternity.

276) Using caffeine or any other medicine is not unpardonable.

277) Thinking that the use of medicine is unpardonable is unpardonable.

278) Using medicine properly is not even a sin, but what is proper is tricky.

279) Good nutrition without medicine or caffeine is the best quality of life when possible.

280) Thinking that sin is unpardonable is unpardonable.

281) The only unpardonable sin is rejecting God-Christ's-Spirit to pardon sin.

282) The only unpardonable sin is thinking that God-Christ's-Spirit cannot pardon sin.

283) The only unpardonable sin is not trusting Christ's Spirit for Heaven's love.

284) The only unpardonable sin is rejecting God's Sons sacrifice for pardoning sin.

285) The only unpardonable sin is rejecting God's Trinitarian power to raise Christ.

286) 7 points above represents the same unpardonable sin of rejecting God eternally.

287) Do I agree with your church? Don't know but can share "Spirit & Truth" as best possible.

288) Churches deserve appreciation for being regular reminders of God-Christ's-Spirit.

289) Opposing redemption is a form of stealing against God.

290) It is not selfish to use caffeine to stay alert while driving at 1 am.

291) Should a person drive at 1 am in the morning? Not usually, but it depends.

292) Being overly selfish comes from the heart not caffeine.

293) Caffeine does not direct selfishness, but causes lack of conscientiousness.

294) Caffeine causes a lack of conscientiousness, stress, and impulsiveness.

295) A person on caffeine can choose to be conscientious, but has to acknowledge the need.

296) It is easier to be conscientious off of caffeine than on caffeine.

297) Some people don't want to be conscientious.

298) Some people have never even noticed they are not conscientious.

299) Strong conscientiousness comes from recognizing I am a sinner.

300) Medium conscientiousness comes from others helping your conscience.

301) Weak conscientiousness comes from agreeing with others who oppose good will.

302) Weak conscientiousness comes from rejecting God in psychology or in full.

303) Weak conscientiousness comes from lack of or no Godly compassion.

304) God gave us a lot in writing instead of yelling, except for thunder.

305) Thunder has a loud voice warning us that death's end is possible.

306) Understanding priority is a discerning of the mind, talents and God's laws.

307) Singing unto Jesus without warnings of Hell is not a belief in Heavens divide.

308) Heavens perfect divide keeps all pain and sorrow out.

309) There is no evidence of any other Heavenly God besides God-Christ's-Spirit.

310) Evidence of God rising from the dead definitively matters.

311) Slavery is stealing, but abortion is murder.

312) A Slave can be freed, but murder ends a life.

313) Should we change the phrase "Stop the Violence" to "Stop The Assaults"?

314) Self-defense is a necessary violence; assault is an ambush or unnecessary fight.

315) New life is given by the one new day's come from.

316) Feed 2 birds with 1 piece of bread.

317) There are dignified and undignified people in all ethnicities.

318) Undignified people start fights with other people and police.

319) Democrat media promotes unsafe behavior around Police.

320) Any civilian should conduct themselves safely around Police.

321) Being neighborly with Police is proper under God and safe for both parties.

322) Christ flew up to Heaven 40 days after His resurrection in front of witnesses.

323) Old Testament Judaism was Christianity's Fetus.

324) Bible preservation was a miracle - even computer work is hard to keep around.

325) Medicines have pros & cons & more cons than pros; use only if highly necessary.

326) The longest location I have lived is inside my mind and body.

327) African slave trade is just as wrong as American slavery.

328) Islamic slave trade is just as wrong as American slavery.

329) Black slave masters are just as wrong as White slave masters.

330) Active slavery today is just as wrong as the "Atlantic Slave Trade".

331) Do not let crooked, lying Scientists work with legislators to empower

drug cartels.

332) Human commonalities are 100% & various experiences do not define humans.

333) True racists oppose the "American Flag", because it defines us as one race from God.

334) Why send someone to war to fight for your family to kill its own baby?

335) It is a joy to be able to cite Hell and tell people they can choose not to go there.

336) Republican style governing respects life.

337) Time flies but never dies, when perceived as slow - learn to grow.

338) Where does Jesus say to be racist? He commands "love your neighbors & enemies."

339) I have never heard a real definition of racism from Democrats.

340) I have never heard a Democrat call an Abortionist racist.

341) Real hope finds ways to introduce the hopeless to Christ.

342) Faith in real hope wants to rescue hopelessness.

343) No human law is above God's laws.

344) Every person is more valuable than Democrat American laws.

345) God is more valuable than Democrat American laws.

346) God's laws don't change.

347) People know how to stay within safe speeds because of Speed Limit laws.

348) Every law is not like a speed limit law, but anger is related to "thou shalt not kill."

349) When we are angry, we look at God's commandments and tap down

that anger.

350) People are above laws in the sense that God's laws exist to support their life.

351) People are not immune from consequences of breaking laws if caught.

352) People are responsible for breaking God's laws if not reconciled through Christ.

353) Believers have eternal reconciliation with Christ.

354) Believers get into Heaven but have to go to court in Heaven.

355) Believers have one court date in Heaven for sins they did not confess in prayer and repent of.

356) Believers lose some rewards in Heaven for unrepentant sins on earth.

357) "The Judgement Seat of Christ" is where believers are tried.
(2 Corinthians 5:10-11; Romans 14:10-12)

358) A baby's body is not the Fathers, Mothers, Sisters or Brothers body.

359) Caffeine increases manic impulsiveness and being scatterbrained.

360) Manic impulsiveness comes from pride and micromanaging.

361) Manic impulsiveness can also come from uncontrolled appetites including emotional.

362) Rebuke Pharisee-ism, which today is called legalism.

363) Knowledge is a map, understanding plans a journey & wisdom loves God.

364) It is impossible to tolerate everything, but forgiveness covers everything.
365) In reality, if you are not a Christian then you are racist.

366) Many blueprints for a better World are in this book.

367) Evolution is racist.

358) Evolution is a racist lie!

359) Democrat mobs do not believe in neighborly justice, truth or God.

360) Put the Bible on a National pedestal.

361) God shows us how to love neighbors via His laws and commands us to follow.

362) Gang initiations / slave branding - What is the difference?

363) Race equality is in line with truth not lies.

364) Race equality comes from one race truth not money.

365) Don't allow baby killing abortion supporters to be Police.

366) Mobs do not respect "due process".

367) "Due process" is too slow today in many cases.

368) Analysis is not irrelevant it observes many possibilities.

369) Objective analysis focuses on unbiased facts.

370) Mobs do not have a formula for neighborly justice - courts do.

371) Democrat media refuses to show real statistics of White people being killed.

372) God's laws apply equally to all ethnicities of people.
373) All false religions are racist.

374) No slavery is good, not Black on Black or White on White.

375) Why do Democrats think it's okay to snitch on a Cop, but not on a murderer in a gang?

376) Systematic racism today ignores evidence of Black assault on Police & blames White people.

377) Systematic racism today ignores White & Black statistic similarities in Police encounters.

378) Systematic racism today ignores Black on White crime statistics, which approximately triple White on Black.

379) Strange things happen when God's commandments are rejected in government.

380) When someone assaults Police & something bad happens - it is their own fault.

381) When someone resists arrest & something bad happens - it is their own fault.

382) Police help at car accidents, and they rescue kidnapped children = valuable.

383) Democrat's systematic racism opposes self-defense for White Americans.

384) Democrat media's systematic hate for America promotes violence on Americans.

385) Violent systematic racism is mostly against Wh te Americans not Black.

386) Systematic racism of media lies is directed toward Black Americans.

387) Systematic racism of media lies is against both White and Black for dividing.

388) Systematic racism promotes violence against White & calls them racist if they address it.

389) Is the violent media promoted racism against Whites to divide or to take White lives?

390) The racist violence media promotes is really intended to silence & kill freedom lovers.

391) Although Democrat media promotes killing Republicans - division is their simultaneous goal.

392) It is not racist to put a White or Black person in jail for stealing.

393) For peacemaking - the approach must be "all lives matter" in a neighborly justice way.

394) Stop Democrats from redefining criminal to being "those who protect you from thieves."

395) People often marginalize the word "criminal" without distinguishing repentant versus unrepentant.

396) Repentant criminals are not the problem; unrepentant criminals are & they legislate legal abortion.

397) If they attack Police - they will attack anyone.

398) Democrat media defends violent aggressors and ignore assault evidence.

399) Citizens should receive a book of current laws.

400) Citizens should have a book of law of how to behave in Police encounters.

SECTION 3:

401) Violence is not racism - people engage in violence for various reasons; self-defense is one valid reason, but assault is absolutely wrong.

402) Violence is a result of temper, pride, hate, no morals, or self-defense.

403) People are supposed to control their tempers and forgive.

404) Exercising self-control for diplomacy versus violence is not uttered by Democrat media.

405) If Democrat media can't silence speech, they push violence - never diplomacy.

406) Republicans condone forgiveness for racists versus Democrats creating more racists.

407) Telling suspects to be peaceful with Police is the compassionate message.

408) Love your racist neighbors should equal "love your enemies."

409) We are all created equally as proven by Noah's Ark carrying the World's only survivors.

410) Everyone came from Noah's family after the flood.

411) Before the flood of Noah's time we all came ecually from God, Adam, and Eve.

412) After the flood God changed language at the "Tower of Babel."

413) Various ethnicities came from God changing language.

414) People groups of the same language moved together to various regions.

415) Resurrected Christ proved His power of Creation, the flood, and language change.

416) Living in different regions engages tissue hormone response variations. (My studied nutrition opinion)

417) Some things we don't know until Heaven, but we know Noah's family is a root connection.

418) Evolution = Racism / Creation = One human race.

419) Women of all ethnicities have the same human menstrual cycle system.

420) All people are clearly people in how we need to do the same hygiene.

421) There are far more evidences of common humanity than differences that represent artistry.

422) The artistry of 2 different paintings still represents painted pictures.

423) The artistry of 2 different personalities in humans still represents

humans & God.

424) The fact that animals also have personalities does not make them human.

425) Animals do not have a soul decision like humans do.

426) Animals cannot discern morals the same way humans are able to.

427) Animals clearly have a type of love and affection.

428) Animals clearly know when they have done wrong when trained.

429) Animals clearly have feelings you are not happy with them.

430) Animals are interesting but incapable of communicating like humans can.

431) Humans are capable of rational communication but bad spirits hinder them.

432) Humans have a choice of spirit versus choosing apathetic spirits.

433) Does apathy value eternal life's ultimatum? No.

434) Apathy does not value life as special, but the apathetic value life's emotions.

435) Many people live according to emotion, and the result is near demonic.

436) Can you tell if someone worships emotions or is demon controlled?

437) One who worships emotion follows any spirit & dastardly fails to revere God's.

438) There are more White people in jail than Black in America. Should they protest?

439) Black lives matter to Marxism? Only a Dictator and ruling class matters in Marxism.

440) Democrat's global supremacy plan is not the answer.

441) How can the Democrats be against supremacists and for global supremacy?

442) White criminals who assault Police need to stay in jail until proven peaceable.

443) Black criminals who assault Police need to stay in jail until proven peaceable.

444) Hispanic criminals who assault Police need to stay in jail until proven peaceable.

445) Anyone who clearly assaults Police needs to stay in jail until proven peaceable.

446) It is racist to say that a White person could never understand a Black person.

447) Black lives matter to drug cartels? Only for money.

448) Lives only matter 100% to Christ.

449) Nobody's life matters 100% to self without trusting Christ.

450) God's forgiveness is sealed in His blood on the cross.

451) Everyone is dying = people never evolve.

452) Christ rose from the dead + visibly ascended toward Heaven.

453) Do not reach for the stars - reach for Christ the Creator of the stars.

454) Love God's give of repentance, eternal salvation and redeeming life.

455) Trust in Christ's Heavenly political quality.

456) One of the best aspects of Heaven is 100% enforced neighborly love.

457) Tolerance is only temporary, but the root of forgiveness is forever.

458) You can study law 24/7 & find nothing better than God's 10 commandments.

459) Human rights to property & life come from God in His commandments.

460) White people matter too.

461) Asian people matter too.

462) Indian people matter too.

463) Hispanic people matter too.

464) Arab people matter too.

465) Mixed people matter too.

466) Black people are not the only people who matter.

467) Guard yourself with God's laws & #1 is God-Christ's-Spirit only as God.

468) G-C-S = God-Christ's-Spirit.

469) True victims can also be true victors forever in Christ.

470) We are all born victims of the sin nature, but with a clear rescuer in Christ.

471) If we don't want Christ as Lord then we want to remain Satan's victim.

472) We do not have to be Satan's victim; trust Christ's forgiveness & 2nd life power.

473) We do not cross paths accidentally = God put us all on the same Earth.

474) Redeeming truth loves souls while condemning lies relish destruction.

475) Real planned parenting acknowledges natural law of Husband & Wife.

476) Do not work hard with great discipline while leading people to Hell.

477) Do not hate God for every idiotic thing people do.

478) Be a savior to yourself by accepting the supreme eternal Savior in Christ.

479) Create "Golden Rule" streets with God-Christ's-Spirit.

480) Life is not a crime - murderous abortion is!

481) Private property rights are more valuable than money.

482) "Thou shalt not murder" is more valuable than money.

483) "Thou shalt not commit adultery" is more valuable than money.

484) "Thou shalt have no other god before me" is more valuable than money.

485) "Love your neighbor as yourself" is more valuable than money.

486) "Thou shalt not lie against your neighbor" is more valuable than money.

487) "Honor your Father and Mother" is more valuable than money.

488) If God's Son does not matter to us then nothing really matters to us.

489) Do not wake up on the wrong side of the dead.

490) If Christ's forgiveness did not exist, neither would people.

491) The condemnation of Hell already exists in the unforgiving heart.

492) The torment of Hell already exists in the unforgiving heart.

493) If we do not love the fruit of the Spirit then we simply love Hell.

494) I am a Christian because I want Heaven not because I am good.

495) Disregarding the giver of life is insanity.

496) Let God's laws be your shrink.

497) Selfishness is not all bad = "love your neighbor as your SELF."

498) We can be as selfish as God's Ten commandments allow.

499) The best selfishness is caring enough about self to choose Heaven.

500) People should take the detour when told Hell is down the road.

501) Love your soul more than your sin.

502) There is no dream greater than Heavens hope in Christ.

503) Believers are not promised tomorrow - the only promise is Heaven.

504) Faith in dung for good odor is not good faith.

505) Faith in dead gods for a 2nd life is not good faith.

506) Faith in resurrected Christ for a 2nd life is good faith.

507) Sand is still sand with or without faith in Christ.

508) Faith is faith and truth is truth.

509) Trusting God-Christ's-Spirit is good faith.

510) Without supreme forgiveness there is no real & lasting religion.

511) True religion can be practiced forever with God's resurrection power.

512) God-Christ's-Spirit is a clarity description of Father, Son & Holy Spirit.

513) The Trinity of Christ is fairly understandable in saying God-Christ's-Spirit.

514) Good Religion = Heavenly Religion = Resurrection power Religion.

515) America has the "Freedom of Religion" not the freedom of false religion.

516) A better World is a more neighborly World with Christ's Spirit & truth.

517) The best World is the 2nd life in Christ.

518) Change for Christ's Kingdom.

519) Christ proved that God is love.

520) Christ's politics matter most.

521) The best concepts help us understand more about God.

522) The most pertinent concepts warn people about Hell and how to escape.

523) Complete insanity = Preferring Hell over Heaven.

524) Complete insanity = Preferring Satan over God-Christ's-Spirit.

525) God desires for everyone to choose Heaven where He hosts.

526) Our top talent is the ability to choose Christ as our God for Heaven.

527) Christ's eternal life is the largest handout in History - accept it.

528) The freedom of speech to discriminate against Hell is infinitely important.

529) Immoral freedom steals - moral freedom protects life.

530) When government makes immorality a law that is tyranny.

531) Discriminate against the Democrats conspiring a fatherless society.

532) We can impeach those who make laws against nature like same sex marriage laws.

533) "The Declaration Of Independence" allows impeaching leaders who impose unnatural law.

534) "The Declaration of Independence" defines us as being under "Creations God."

535) "The Declaration of Independence" defines us as one human race from God.

536) Without gratefulness you never had anything - it had you.

537) Ungratefulness causes wealthy to think they have nothing to give.

538) Don't steal from yourself with unrealistic expectations that steal time.

539) Do not steal monetary redemption rights from people.

540) Do not steal from children by supporting media marriage law lies.

541) Think healthy - your well-being and quality of life matters.

542) Common bigotry stereotypes your whole life story before age 20.

543) Adults seldom get graded properly like tests do in school.

544) Words matter = God had Adam name the animals.

545) The best street fighters are mostly dead or significantly wounded.

546) A big mind is still very limited and a small mind is still vast.

547) Oftentimes, I disagree with everyone and myself.

548) Impressions change with Seasons.

549) Worship Christ not the Bible - The Bible's purpose is to show us Christ.

550) Gospel music never expires.

551) Intimate affection for Gospel music is supernatural through loving God.

552) Meditating with Gospel music is a good way to pray.

553) Money does not last but can count towards Heaven.

554) Make money count eternally.

555) Don't count on money, make it count for Heaven.

556) Perception is what we see with our minds eye.

557) Patience while waiting for understanding is infinitely valuable.

558) Moral freedom opens doors for truth over lies.

559) Be a "Misconception Non-Conformist" to worldly things.

560) Be a "Misconception Non-Conformist" in Christ's Spirit and truth.

561) Be a non-conformist to anti-Christ spirits.

562) Be a non-conformist to murdering unborn babies.

563) Be a non-conformist to government degrading natural parenthood.

564) Be a non-conformist to unnatural marriage laws that disrespect God.

565) Be a non-conformist to racist Evolution's lie.

566) Conform to God's creation of one human race from Adam and Eve.

567) Conform to Christ's salvation offer for the entire Human race.

568) Conform to Christ's resurrection power as Lord of eternity.

569) God's laws are for correction, direction & protection not destruction.

570) Christ's forgiveness is the most valuable forgiveness.

571) Pro Heaven poetry cares.

572) Misconceptions are born from lies and can be cleared up with truth.

573) Wash your brain with truth.

574) Brainwash yourself with Christ's eternally clean water.

575) Repentant truth pursuit is representative of walking with Heaven's peace.

576) A perspective of comfort is valid with hope in Christ.

577) The grass is truly viewed as more pleasant with the fruit of the Spirit.

578) Holy love is seen in Christ's forgiveness, and taught in the believing hearts soul.

579) Valuable faith believes in the proven Heaven with streets of gold.

580) Christ proved Heaven with His resurrection and ascension.

581) Give people a peace piece of Heaven with Christ's words and Spirit.

582) Support the reality of men's and women's existence as created by God.

583) The reality of existence accepted in creation's form is a peace-loving contentment.

584) A nation disregarding God's commandments is experiencing a sample of Hell.

585) Prayer for the mind = 'Dear God-Christ's-Spirit direct my mind.'

586) Robots can be programmed according to ethics, but cannot make an ethical decision.

587) Anyone can change - Trust Christ's forgiveness & keep learning more from God.

588) Some people behave worse than wild animals, but they are not animals.

589) People are often highly trained in people pleasing, but God pleasing takes priority.

590) A nation honoring God's laws gives citizens a taste of Heaven.

591) Valuing God's laws is key to keeping slavery from slipping in.

592) Democrats call people racist & also claim pregnant women aren't carrying humans.

593) The Human race did not come separately.

594) Various languages sound different, but communicate the same general things.

595) Enlightening against mass deception takes trust in the power of planting truth.

596) We plant the seeds of truth and Spirit - God grows the seeds.

597) People relations matter as part of God's 2nd greatest command.

598) The free-market system loves its employees by design.

599) Democrats think it is okay to offend Christ, but not dead gods.

600) Do not go against the only risen living God - go against the false
ones.

SECTION 4:

601) Having dislike for rotten food is rational, but dislike for healthy food is
not.

602) Even opossums know bumping into a wall indicates the wrong
direction.

603) Choosing evil can blur the recognition of peaceful order as peaceful.

604) There should be public reverence for Godly laws, which are
neighborly laws.

605) Private reverence for God and His laws is a decision of each heart.

606) There is no getting around that God's laws are the most neighborly.

607) Everyone knows that the right way to govern is with neighborly laws.
608) Corrupt government uses greedy criminal groups to oppose peace.

609) People understand God's laws but some choose greed and hate.

610) There is no real peace and order with liars who hate God's laws.

611) Purpose to exodus when recognizing deception ASAP.

612) Class love does not get you into Heaven - loving God does.

613) Direction matters more than speed - the wrong direction is no good.

614) Learn to earn for Heaven's sake and your work will not be a waste.

615) Be an infinite child of life not destruction.

616) Believe that death is everyone's path who does not trust Christ's path.

617) Do not be dependent on imperfection for spiritual hope.

618) Receptive learning accepts that we don't know everything.

619) The evolutionist KKK burned crosses in hate of Christ & His forgiveness.

620) It is obvious Evolutionists had a role in corrupting medicine.

621) No one needs to be an academic genius to believe in Christ as Lord.

622) The clearest part of the Bible is the most important = Trust Christ.

623) Understanding the Bible comes from staying focused on the themes.

624) Outlaw baby fetus human being slaughterhouses.

625) Stand up stretch your spiritual muscles.

626) Breathe Christ's oxygen.

627) Talk tactfully and confidently let people know where life comes from.

628) Without the gift of repentance, we would be stuck with Satan.

629) Your natural anatomy matters.

630) Wisdom is better than any human IQ & anyone can choose it.

631) Forgiveness has a cause greater than our preference.

632) Murder is not a green light to give to government - outlaw abortion.

633) Truth is a quest not a jest for vain intimidation.

634) Life is a gift; gifts are for enjoyment.

635) Jesus is my excuse for doing good.

636) Forgiveness is precursor & part of "loving neighbors as yourself."

637) Loving God is a prerequisite for "loving neighbors as yourself."

638) Christ redeems the repentant outcast.

639) Bigotry and stereotyping are faiths that lead to Hell.

640) Christianity is the religion of truth in action at the cross.

641) Refrain from one who refuses to resolve while pretending to forgive.

642) If you cannot refrain from the begrudged continue to forgive them.

643) Continual forgiveness leans on patience and hope for your own peace.

644) Remember to pray for your enemy when needing to forgive repetitiously.

645) We should hope our enemy trusts Christ's truth, Spirit & salvation.

646) Pray for enemies, even if they are a supposed Christian holding a grudge.

647) Pray that a supposed Christian is awakened to choose and trust Spirit peace.

648) Pray for an unsaved enemy to enjoy being at peace with you and to trust Christ.

649) A daily forgiveness outlook is the way of eternal life.

650) Direct repeated forgiving is sometimes needed along with standard heart forgiveness.

651) Forgiving allows peace and order, but does not mean to concur with evil.

652) Forgiving is orderly, and is proper whether we are able to resist conflict or not.

653) Forgiveness does not ignore just reconciliation, but allows a

measured resolve.

654) Forgiveness allows for a measured and fair resolution or for a pardon.

655) In modern times many do not deeply understand reconciling and resolution.

656) Patience is a valuable Holy Spirit fruit, which enables harmony amid conflict.

657) Today, we chase being busy, but real productivity compliments evangelism.

658) True productivity does not stuff Spirit and truth into a drawer.

659) I can think of nothing more productive than walking in the Spirit at all times.

660) Walking in the Spirit can be a challenging mindset during labor and pressure.

661) Walking in the Spirit can succeed by focusing on a fruit like temperance.

662) Temperance, hope, faith and Heavenly compassion help Spirit mindfulness.

663) Spirit mindfulness is supremely productive from sharing God's fruit.

664) Spirit mindfulness is productive from others experiencing God's fruit.

665) Spirit fruit speaks in more ways than words can via emotions & liberty.

666) Spirit fruit comes from Christ's Spirit and speaks to the heart, soul & mind.

667) Spirit mindfulness helps a person to do menial tasks more efficiently.

668) Efficiency is often disrupted by fear and stress in feeling overwhelmed.

669) Fear & panic over many tasks do not engage durable energy, Spirit does.

670) Both God's Holy Spirit & Human survival spirit are fluid in a calm mind.

671) There are explanations deep in our psyche that tell us how to succeed.

672) We often do not recognize the explanation of how our psyche works.

673) Our psyche tells us to do a task calmly.

674) Our psyche tells us to speed up when it knows we are coordinated vs manic.

675) Our psyche tells us when to work steadily and orderly for endurance efficiency.

676) Even non-Christian psyche can work sound & orderly via survival instinct.

677) An unbeliever can learn principles that help survival just like a believer can.

678) An unbeliever may gravitate more than a believer to what works for survival.

679) When an unbeliever finds what works for them, that is all they have.

680) Sometimes what brings success to unbelievers blinds them even more.

681) Unbelievers do not have the hope of Heaven.

682) There is a downside to human success in that there is no real peace in it.

683) There is a downside to human success in that there is no future in it.

684) There is a downside to human success in that one may feel no need for God.

685) There is a downside to human success in fearing that God would interrupt it.

686) Human success can obsess with self-gratification and not see the big picture.

687) There is always more to see in the big picture, but some don't see it at all.

688) The big visionary picture of eternity has a lens given by Christ's evidence.

689) The big visionary picture of Heaven gives more purpose to work not less.

690) Having a visionary picture of Heaven gives survival work value.

691) We need to trust resurrected Christ for the bigger picture over our plans.

692) God is God and we are not - we could die any day.

693) Put your eternal life in God's hands.

694) Getting good advice from other people is often rare and sometimes never.

695) Why is good advice rare in America? Because, people are busy in success.

696) Why is good advice rare? People's tendency is to think their way is the only way.

697) Why is good advice rare? People have only seen what works for them.

698) Why is good advice rare? Some people simply don't know or don't care.

699) Encouraging words with the intent of encouraging go a long way.

700) You can fathom people don't have the solution = True encouragement matters.

701) People will say an encouraging word to brush someone off & not encourage.

702) Everyone is called by God to be a real encourager = "love your neighbor."

703) Having God's expectation for others to be kind can be discouraging.

704) There will be some genuine encouragers and more discouragers.

705) Make sure you fall into the bracket of true neighborly encourager.

706) We are limited and can only encourage someone now and then.

707) We cannot always have the right words, except in various settings.

708) Standing for proper orderliness and political structure is mass encouraging.

709) People come together in Church and are able to mass encourage.

710) There are multiple encouraging messages within a Church setting.

711) In Church people hear a sermon, sing together, recognize human equality...

712) In Church people are in a comforting humble setting celebrating God.
713) Being verbally supportive of Churches encourages many by helping Church.

714) People have quirks but Churches commemorating God highlights redemption.

715) Being human is actually comforting to realize and Church is humble comfort.

716) Humble comfort as a human being enjoys the preeminent comfort of God.

717) God is just, merciful, and preparing a place of perfect peace for His people.

718) Set your measure and feeling aside and have policy that enables success.

719) Do not begrudge individual management based on one's short change management results.

720) If individuals mismanage, encourage them to learn to hold on to what is theirs.

721) Let private life mismanaging continue until one learns versus disqualifying managing.

722) Private property rights must be respected even for disorderly managers.

723) We cannot make excuses for discouraging private property rights.

724) We cannot make excuses for opposing any individual property rights.

725) A lender should grant payment flexibility.

726) Society's enforcement methodology for debtor's should be solid.

727) Payment contracts should be re-adjusted for loyal payees short of funds.

728) Christ's reconciliation principles apply in business dealings.

729) Christ's principles work better for relations than academic training.

730) Supernatural reconciliation helps business via valuing life.

731) Business is not a lounge and needs boundaries.

732) Business can have strict boundaries and support compassionate Churches.

733) Business can have strict boundaries on the job and support local shelters.

734) Business is helped by valuing private property rights for housing.

735) There is no shelter better than private property rights.

736) Competing and complicating homeownership access is not productive.

737) Competition complicating homeownership access is not humane.

738) Competition complicating homeownership affordability hurts society.

739) Less homeownership = more desperate, stressed and angry people.

740) Private land and home property owned by banks should have more rent to own options.

741) Private land and home property owned by banks should have reasonable down payments.

742) Private land and home property for sale should be priced at the private owner's discretion.

743) The banked owned property should offer attainable deals.

744) Private owned property should be sold at whatever price they want.

745) It is better to sell a property for a reasonable price than finding no buyers.

746) It is better to rent reasonably priced than to have no renter at all.

747) Today, people have numerous bills and can pay a rent but not a security deposit.

748) Is sticking to a security deposit requirement worth having zero renters? No.

749) Solid rules are helpful, but no grace and flexibility grow's poverty.

750) When poverty grows it harms the full circle.

751) God's laws are not only peaceful and eternal - they make mathematical sense.

752) God's laws mathematically help a nation full circle.

753) God's laws help to bring more peace and order full circle.

754) When things are going better, corrupt media lies as if they aren't - to make them worse.

755) Corrupt media lies when things are going bad to make it seem better.

756) Don't base your politics on what seems good, base them on God's laws.

757) Remember Christ's "Golden Rule" of treating others fairly and humanely.

758) What part of "love your neighbor as yourself" does not mean to be fair?

759) We can see the stars but the stars cannot see us.

760) Christianity is the Religion of truth in action at resurrection.

761) Christianity is the Religion of love in action at Christ's cross forgiveness.

762) Christianity is the Religion of truth versus chaotic lies.

763) Christianity is the Religion of everlasting peace.

764) Christianity is the Religion of redeeming peace on Earth.
765) Christianity is the Religion of reconciling peace and neighborly order.

766) Democrats hate women so much they want to replace them with men in wigs.

767) Assess your own motives regularly.

768) We are human "under God."

769) Good thespianism is the non-fiction mirror of eternal living internalized.

770) Rise with Christ not with your own ceiling.

771) We all have more than one eye cue + IQ.

772) Value other people's labor not just your own.

773) Sharing Christ = Sharing supreme forgiveness.

774) Without Fathers - Mothers do not even exist.

775) Sanity's boredom = Insanity's door.

776) Gender destruction is not a neighborly Science and should be outlawed.

777) Houses with walls are some of the best things in existence.

778) Property with fences is very accommodating for pets and children.

779) Homes are built to be lived in.

780) Discrimination is necessary - Discriminate against crossing busy streets.

781) Love is creative.

782) Biblical Human Genesis came from a preeminently creative Artist.

783) Compassion does not come from a self-righteous dead end.

784) True compassion comes from faith in lasting hope.
785) I prefer to say I am happy instead of proud.

786) Pride is a root sin according to Christ's Bible.

787) An over achiever often feels like an under achiever.

788) Be a complete achiever by committing labor to Heaven's gain.

789) Labor is not vanity when your earnings help share God's hope.

790) Labor is not vanity when you remember to walk in truth and Spirit.

791) Labor is not vanity when you find ways to relate God's peace.

792) Labor is not vanity when you work for survival and trust in the Lord.

793) Labor is a necessary part of life, but we can make it count eternally.

794) God-Christ's-Spirit created politics - get discernment with Him.

795) Stolen items can be paid back, but a stolen life cannot.

796) Do you have God's Spirit of "love, power and sound mind"?
(2 Timothy 1:7)

797) Do you have God's loving compassion, forgiveness and redemption?

798) Notice what works = unforgiveness kills - forgiveness sustains.

799) My Christian belief influenced me to view strangers as human neighbors.

800) Words beyond words are in the Spirit realm.

SECTION 5:

801) Walking with God's Spirit is the best way to "redeem the time."

802) Have patience - "In Spirit and in truth."
803) Have love - "In Spirit and in truth."
804) Have joy - "In Spirit and in truth."
805) Have peace - "In Spirit and in truth."
806) Have meekness - "In Spirit and in truth."
807) Have goodness - "In Spirit and in truth."
808) Have gentleness - "In Spirit and in truth."
809) Have faith - "In Spirit and in truth."
810) Have temperance - "In Spirit and in truth."
811) Have power - "In Spirit and in truth."
813) Have a sound mind - "In Spirit and in truth."
814) Have confidence - "In Spirit and in truth."
815) Have understanding - "In Spirit and in truth."
816) Have reconciliation - "In Spirit and in truth."
817) Have intercession - "In Spirit and in truth."
818) Have righteousness - "In Spirit and in truth."
819) Have purity - "In Spirit and in truth."
820) Have compassion - "In Spirit and in truth."
821) Have rewards - "In Spirit and in truth."

822) Plant seeds - "In Spirit and in truth."
823) Do works - "In Spirit and in truth."
824) Forgive repeatedly - "In Spirit and in truth."
825) Give mercy - "In Spirit and in truth."
826) Repent regularly - "In Spirit and in truth."
827) Teach repentance - "In Spirit and in truth."
828) Share Christ's eternal salvation - "In Spirit and in truth."
829) Share Christ's grace - "In Spirit and in truth."
830) Extend Christ's redemption - "In Spirit and in truth."
831) Pray - "In Spirit and in truth."
832) Love God - "In Spirit and in truth."
833) "Love your neighbor as yourself" - "In Spirit and in truth."
834) Love God's counsel - "In Spirit and in truth."
835) Love God's Disciples - "In Spirit and in truth."
836) Love enemies - "In Spirit and in truth."
837) Love Christians - "In Spirit and in truth."
838) Love Baby Christians - "In Spirit and in truth."
839) Love hypocrites - "In Spirit and in truth."
840) Love Pharisees - "In Spirit and in truth."
841) Love legalists - "In Spirit and in truth."
842) Love the whole World - "In Spirit and in truth."
843) Hate vanity - "In Spirit and in truth."
844) Hate sin - "In Spirit and in truth."
845) Hate death - "In Spirit and in truth."
846) Hate Hell - "In Spirit and in truth."
847) Hate lies - "In Spirit and in truth."
848) Love repentance - "In Spirit and in truth."
849) Love Godly justice - "In Spirit and in truth."
850) Encourage people - "In Spirit and in truth."
851) Love redemptive justice - "In Spirit and in truth."
852) Judge discerningly - "In Spirit and in truth."
853) Be reconciling - "In Spirit and in truth."
854) Distribute redeeming justice - "In Spirit and in truth."
855) Oppose condemning justice - "In Spirit and in truth."
856) Oppose injustice - "In Spirit and in truth."
857) Comfort people - "In Spirit and in truth."
858) "Go ye into all the World" - "In Spirit and in truth."

859) I am not sure who is a hypocrite except in extreme cases.

860) An example of an extreme hypocrite is a pro-abortion Pastor.

861) An example of true hypocrisy is a Bible Pastor who condones Islam.

862) The love that many have for Gospel music is supernatural.

863) Desiring to learn more about God is supernatural.

864) Christ rising from the dead is supernatural.

865) Christ's forgiveness on the cross is supernatural.

866) Be wise and simplify things.

867) Christianity keeps me youthfully exploring what God knows.

868) Crucifixion is celebrated on a Friday, in April each year.

869) Crucifixion day is a big celebration day of forgiveness for you and me.

870) Do not sorrow at Christ's crucifixion as if there is no hope.

871) Sorrow at Christ's crucifixion for the pain He suffered for our sin nature.

872) Let Christ be your Lord not your sin nature.

873) Celebrate Christ's forgiveness because He later rose from the dead.

874) School tried to make me smart - God compels me to be real.
875) If you want to go to Hell - don't trouble other people with it.

876) Do not play "Devil's advocate." Why not be God's advocate?

877) Politicians who facilitate abortion should get the death penalty.

878) We should treasure repentance like gold from Heaven.

879) Baby killers do not care about women.

880) Jesus rested in a grave on Sabbath day? Significant? Rest.

881) Jesus was crucified for not denying He is God.

882) Jesus was dead 2 nights and 1 1/4 day or so.

883) Resurrection was actually day 3 from when crucifixion started.

884) If it is not of Jesus - it is of Hell.

885) God's grace works against many bad spirits.

886) All who crucified Jesus are dead, but He is still alive.

887) Encourage redemption.
888) Encourage restoration.
889) Encourage reconciliation.
890) Encourage forgiveness.
891) Encourage eternal salvation.
892) Encourage repentance.
893) Encourage neighborliness.
894) Encourage peacemaking.
895) Encourage diplomacy.
896) Encourage neighborly justice.
897) Encourage moral freedom.
898) Encourage private prayer.
899) Encourage genuine prayer.
900) Encourage natural Fatherhood.
901) Encourage natural Motherhood.
902) Encourage natural Parenthood.
903) Encourage natural marriage.
904) Encourage natural parent responsibility.
905) Encourage natural family adoption.
906) Encourage private property rights.
907) Encourage redemptive justice.
908) Encourage discernment.
909) Encourage wisdom.
910) Encourage truth.
911) Encourage Christ's "Golden Rule."
912) Encourage eternal compassion.
913) Encourage sober mindedness.
914) Encourage vigilance.
915) Encourage Godly loving pursuits.
916) Encourage pursuit of righteousness.
917) Encourage patience.
918) Encourage temperance.
919) Encourage Spirit and truth worship.
920) Encourage eternal faith.

921) Encourage resurrection faith.
922) Encourage eternal joy.
923) Encourage Christ's hope.
924) Encourage mercy.
925) Encourage eternal hope.
926) Encourage meekness.
927) Encourage revering God.
928) Encourage truth pursuit.
929) Encourage loving God.
930) Encourage God's laws.
931) Encourage understanding "Under God."
932) Encourage Godly focus.
933) Encourage charity.
934) Encourage stewardship.
935) Encourage appetite temperance.
936) Encourage being Spirit-filled.
937) Encourage property protection.
938) Encourage Biblical meditation.

939) Stop hallucinating evolution.

940) God wants everyone.

941) Conception is sacred.

942) Umbilical cord is a sovereign evidenced lifeline.
943) Choose Christ's Heaven not Hell.
944) Choose Heavens power, not your own.
945) Choose repentance.
946) Choose Humility "under God."

947) Trust revelation faith.
948) Trust God's baby revelation.
949) Trust God's cross forgiveness revelation.
950) Trust God's ascension power revelation.
951) Choose God's ascension power revelation.
952) Choose God's cross forgiveness revelation.

953) Love your mate not abortion.

954) Christ proved that He is God.

955) "Under God" = under true wisdom.

956) Defund Evolution.

957) Loves label = Jesus Christ.

958) Proper population control = honoring God's ten commandments.

959) Evolution is racist!

960) Outlaw the racist Evolution theory.

961) Abolish Evolution.

962) Outlaw Evolution.

963) Ban Evolution in Schools.

964) Teach Creation's equality not Evolution.

965) Teach one human race from God, Adam and Eve not Evolution.

966) Animalistic Evolution is not human equality.

967) We did not evolve unequally from animals.

968) God created human equality.
969) God created one human race.
970) God created human anatomy.
971) God created gender.
972) God created you through His pro-creation.

973) Plan natural parenthood.
974) True planned parenthood loves babies.
975) Plan Fatherhood + Motherhood.

976) I am an Independence Globalist under God-Christ's-Spirit.

977) Natural parenthood matters.
978) Real Doctors save lives.
979) Babies are human.
980) Abortion is murder.
981) Abolish abortion, outlaw abortion, outlaw Abortionists.
982) Outlaw Abortion Clinics.

983) A womb is not a tomb.
984) A womb = a child's first room.

985) Celebrate Lincoln's victory.
986) Celebrate Republicans outlawing slavery, in 1865.
987) February is a good time to Celebrate Lincoln's victory over slavery.

988) Trust Heavens quality.
989) Property rights matter.
990) Border security matters.
991) C-C-S saves.

992) Satan works for evil - work for good.

993) Life is not a crime.

994) Wisdom walks with forgiveness.
995) Life would not exist without forgiveness.
996) Extreme insanity rejects Christ.
997) Hell is unforgiving; choose forgiveness.

998) A better World works wisely.
999) The best World = the next one.
1000) Faith's source matters.

1001) Understand God.
1002) Moral freedom protects life.
1003) Immoral freedom steals.
1004) God's politics matter.

1005) Gratefulness acknowledges positivity.

1006) Don't steal your peace with God.

1007) God-Christ's-Spirit is the cause of faith.
1008) Faith in dirt for the 2nd life is no good.
1009) Faith in dead gods is no good.

1010) Defy stereotyping - life is not over before 20.

1011) The human mind is vast.

1012) Pray with Gospel music.

1013) For higher learning disagree with yourself.

1014) Believing "all have sinned" points to God as supreme.

1015) Money burns as will its lovers.

1016) Be a non-conformist to Satan.
1017) Be a non-conformist to misconceptions.
1018) Be a non-conformist to Abortionists.
1019) Be a non-conformist to marriage perversions.
1020) Be a non-conformist to Evolution's lies.
1021) Be a non-conformist to destruction.
1022) Be a non-conformist to hating people.
1023) Be a non-conformist to common bigotry.
1024) Be a non-conformist to doubting God.
1025) Be a non-conformist to staying depressed.
1026) Be a non-conformist to pessimism.
1027) Be a non-conformist to fantasies.
1028) Be a non-conformist to delusions.
1029) Be a non-conformist to lies.
1030) Be a non-conformist to slander.
1031) Be a non-conformist to defamation.
1032) Be a non-conformist to false witness.
1033) Be a non-conformist to oppression.
1034) Be a non-conformist to shaming.
1035) Be a non-conformist to chaos.
1036) Be a non-conformist to violence.
1037) Be a non-conformist to stealing.
1038) Be a non-conformist to drunkenness.
1039) Be a non-conformist to over punishing.
1040) Be a non-conformist to revenge.
1041) Be a non-conformist to injustice.
1042) Be a non-conformist to bitterness.
1043) Be a non-conformist to stressful thoughts.
1044) Be a non-conformist to unnecessary stress.
1045) Be a non-conformist to unhealthy stress.
1046) Be a non-conformist to gluttony.
1047) Be a non-conformist to vanity.
1048) Be a non-conformist to true racism.
1049) Be a non-conformist to rejecting Christ.
1050) Be a non-conformist to Hell's destiny.
1051) Be a non-conformist to bad spirits.

1052) Be a non-conformist to mockery.
1053) Be a non-conformist to scorning.
1054) Be a non-conformist to Godless religions.

1055) Godless religion is not Religion.

1056) Be restorative with God-Christ's-Spirit.
1057) Be real with God-Christ's-Spirit.
1058) Be reconciling with God-Christ's-Spirit.
1059) Be forgiving with God-Christ's-Spirit.
1060) Be merciful with God-Christ's-Spirit.
1061) Be encouraging with God-Christ's-Spirit.
1062) Be hopeful with God-Christ's-Spirit.
1063) Be peaceful with God-Christ's-Spirit.
1064) Be good with God-Christ's-Spirit.
1065) Be humble under God-Christ's-Spirit.
1066) Be graceful with God-Christ's-Spirit.
1067) Be gentle with God-Christ's-Spirit.
1068) Be patient with God-Christ's-Spirit.
1069) Be loving with God-Christ's-Spirit.
1070) Be joyful with God-Christ's-Spirit.
1071) Be confident in God-Christ's-Spirit.
1072) Have faith in God-Christ's-Spirit.
1073) Trust in God-Christ's-Spirit.

1074) Be confident in Heavens Christ.
1075) Lean on Christ's truth.
1076) Lean on Christ's resurrection power.
1077) Lean on Christ's forgiveness.
1078) Lean on Christ's salvation.
1079) Lean on Christ's redemption.
1080) Lean on Christ's reconciliation.

1081) Follow Christ's Spirit.

1082) Repent of violent thoughts via love for "thou shalt not kill."
1083) Repent and follow God's ten commandments.
1084) Repent and ask God's forgiveness.

1085) Be forgiven with God-Christ's-Spirit.

1086) Follow God's fruit of the Spirit.
1087) Trust God's fruit of the Spirit.

1088) Have confidence in God's fruit of the Spirit.

1089) Christians are able to think of God in 3 basic Trinitarian ways.
1090) Part of God's personality is learned with the Father, Son & Holy Spirit.

1091) Walk in obedience to the Spirit via the fruit of the Spirit.

1092) God's will is for all to walk with the fruit of the Spirit.
1093) God's will is for all to be confident in Christ for eternal life.
1094) God's will is for all to joy & share in Christ's salvation.
1095) God's will is for all to love & follow to His commandments.
1096) God's will is for all to succeed with His commandments.

1097) Walk in success with God's commandments.
1098) Walk in success with the fruit of the Spirit.
1099) Walk in success with God-Christ's-Spirit.
1100) Walk with love for God's laws.

1101) God-Christ's-Spirit saved me from Hell.
1102) Christ's salvation saves from Hell for eternal life.

1103) Conform to God's commandments.
1104) Conform to God-Christ's-Spirit.
1105) Conform to Heavenly value.
1106) Conform to eternal wealth.
1107) Conform to Eternal value.
1108) Conform to everlasting life.
1109) Conform to reconciliation.
1110) Conform to God's love.
1111) Conform to Spirit and truth.
1112) Conform to Christ's hope.
1113) Conform to Christ's forgiveness.
1114) Conform to Christ's compassion.
1115) Conform to God's peace.
1116) Conform to everlasting peace.
1117) Conform to pure Godly love.
1118) Conform to everlasting love.
1119) Conform to eternal resurrection power.

1120) Conform to loving enemies.
1121) Conform to patience with enemies.
1122) Conform to not envying enemies.

1123) Conform to being kind to enemies.
1124) Conform to praying eternal salvation for enemies.
1125) Conform to Godly hope for enemies.
1126) Conform to forgiving enemies pardon or not.
1127) Conform to Godly justice for enemies.
1128) Conform to fair justice for enemies.
1129) Conform to justice versus revenge for enemies.

1130) Hope for salvation for enemies.
1131) Hope for repentance for enemies.
1132) Pray for salvation for enemies.
1133) Pray for spiritual awakening for enemies.
1134) Pray for God's peace for enemies.
1135) Hope for God's peace for enemies.
1136) Pray for wisdom in dealing with enemies.
1137) Pray that enemies find spiritual wisdom.
1138) Pray that God gives you patience with enemies.
1139) Pray for a spiritual awakening for enemies.
1140) Pray for safety with enemies.
1141) Pray for protection from enemies.
1142) Have defensive protection from enemies.

1143) Conform to seeking wisdom.
1144) Conform to being discerning.
1145) Conform to sharing Christ's ways.
1146) Conform to sharing Christ's salvation.
1147) Conform to warning people about the next life.
1148) Conform to warning people about Hell.
1149) Conform to sharing Heaven's choice.

1150) Don't know who is friend or foe - pray spiritual enlightening for both.

1151) Pro-Heaven music cares.

1152) Forgiveness from Christians comes from God.

1153) Give people a little bit of Heaven with Spirit fruit.
1154) Give people a little bit of Heaven.
1155) Give people Heaven's link = resurrected Christ.

1156) Christ was predestined to offer forgiveness to everyone.

1157) Gender destruction is not self-love.

1158) Following God's law diminishes personal problems.

1159) Government following God's laws diminishes public problems.

1160) Dear God - change my mind.
1161) Dear God - give me wisdom.
1162) Dear God - give me strength.
1163) Dear God - give me temperance.
1164) Dear God - give me joy.
1165) Dear God - give me endurance.
1166) Dear God - give me patience.
1167) Dear God - help my memory.
1168) Dear God - intercede for me.
1169) Dear God - help me.
1170) Dear God - help my focus.
1171) Dear God - enlighten blinded hearts.
1172) Dear God - awaken apathetic hearts.
1173) Dear God - awaken stubborn hearts.
1174) Dear God - enlighten hateful hearts.
1175) Dear God - enlighten unsaved souls.
1176) Dear God - help me redeem time.

1177) Only God is supreme.
1178) Democrats government supremacy goals are not neighborly.
1179) Democrats global supremacy scheme is not neighborly.
1180) Robots have no free will.

1181) Christ is above all gods.
1182) No God except Christ's Trinity.

1183) Anyone can become more Heavenly with Christ.

1184) Positive change takes diligence.
1185) Positive change takes persistence.
1186) Positive change takes patience.
1187) Positive change takes believing Christ not His doubters.
1188) Positive change resists vanity.
1189) Positive change confesses sin to God-Christ's-Spirit.
1190) Positive change acknowledges sin to God-Christ's-Spirit.
1191) Positive change repents regularly.
1192) Positive change wants God's forgiveness.
1193) Positive change wants God's salvation.

1194) Positive change seeks daily communion with G-C-S.
1195) Positive change views people as created in God's image.
1196) Positive change extends God's grace to His enemies.

1197) God's enemies are my enemies.
1198) God's human enemies are my neighbors but also my enemies.
1199) Satan is God's enemy and is my enemy.
1200) Satan is the enemy of God and Christians.
1201) Satan is the enemy of eternal life.
1202) Satan is the enemy of people having a good life.
1203) Satan is the enemy of people who live for truth.
1204) Satan is where lies come from.
1205) Do not be loving lies and following Satan into Hell.

SECTION 7:

1206) True genius actions connect to reality.
1207) True genius actions connect to truth.
1208) Anyone can be the child of preeminent Genius through Christ.
1209) True genius actions acknowledge God consistently.
1210) True genius actions acknowledge God eternally.
1211) True genius actions acknowledge Christ as King of Kings.
1212) True genius actions disagree with self often and reassess.
1213) True genius actions agree with God.
1214) True genius actions agree with God's laws.
1215) True genius connects to God - foolishness does not tune in.
1216) True genius starts with revering God = wisdom. (Proverbs 9:10-12)
1217) God is the preeminent Genius.

1218) Stop forcing dead gods on people.
1219) You cannot offend dead gods.
1220) Stop offending the only living God in Christ.

1221) Opposing deception comes from reverence for truth.

1222) The human race does not come separately - no batteries needed.

1223) Democrats are not racist & Fathers can be Mothers - both wrong.

1224) Please God more than people.

1225) God's #1 rule = love God.

1226) God's #2 rule = love people. (Matthew 22:37-39)

1227) Choose good over evil & eternal pleasure over pain.

1228) Unforgiveness is weird.

1229) Choose golden streets.

1230) Oppose conceptual lies.

1231) Declare and share conceptual truth.
1232) Declare and share spiritual blessings.

1233) Spiritual blessings come from trust in Christ's peace.

1234) Conceptual truth comes from meditating on the Bible.

1235) Temperance reaps peace.

1236) Balancing emotions for God's Spirit and truth brings peace.

1237) Balancing appetites gives more peace.

1238) God's laws are a piece of Heaven.

1239) The Free-Market System allows us to choose and change jobs.

1240) We can only get hired on a job if there is a job available.

1241) We can get hired on a job if the manager thinks we can do the job well.

1242) There are usually plenty of jobs available in America's system.

1243) Republican philosophy has reverence for God & life.
1244) Republican philosophy has reverence for God & truth.

1245) Democrats have no respect for God or life.
1246) Democrats have no respect for God or truth.

1247) Hating God is not a philosophy.
1248) Hating God is a hate for life and reason.

1240) Love reconciliation from Christ and His reconciliation ways.

1241) I am a pro not a con.
1242) I am a child of life not destruction.
1243) I am a child of life not deaths chains.
1244) I am a child of true freedom not bondage to sin.
1245) I am a child of unending hope not oppression.
1246) I am a child of unending hope not hopelessness.
1247) I am a child of infinite hope.
1248) I am a child of resurrection power hope.
1249) I am a child of Christ's forgiveness.
1250) I am a child of Christ's mercy.
1251) I am a child of Christ's grace.
1252) I am a child of Christ's eternal gift.
1253) I am a child of Christ's love.
1254) I am a child of Christ's resurrection.
1255) I am a child of Christ's ascension.
1256) I am a child of transfiguration.
1257) I am a child of Christ's plan.
1258) I am a child of Christ's eternal will.

1259) Resist misconceptions.

1260) Stop stereotyping Republicans.

1261) Love your Republican neighbor.
1262) Love your Democrat enemy of life.
1263) Love bigoted people with forgiveness and truth.

1264) Dead gods can't save.
1265) Dead gods can't forgive.
1266) Dead gods don't bring another day.

1267) Forgiveness does not exist without Christ's Bible.

1268) Christ is my excuse for every good effort.
1269) Christ is my excuse for writing this book.

1270) My excuse for being a loser?
1271) My excuse for what? Doing better than scorners?

1272) Life is a gift; gifts are for enjoyment.

1273) Truth is a quest not a jest for vain intimidation.

1274) Love your Democrat enemy of life with forgiveness & truth.

1275) Wisdom is better than IQ.

1276) Anyone can choose wisdom.

1277) Our souls need to change; our gender is what it is.

1278) Life came from Christ - believe it.
1279) Life comes from Christ - believe it.
1280) Life's transfiguration comes from Christ after death.
1281) Life's transformation is a daily chosen awareness of Christ's will.

1282) Forgiveness is for a greater cause.
1283) Forgiveness is loving.
1284) Forgiveness opens the door to Heaven for one to recognize.

1285) Murderous abortion is not proper power for government.

1286) Christ redeems anyone who believes.
1287) Christ is patient and merciful but tomorrow is not guaranteed.

1288) Godly compassion is not a sin.

1289) Jesus is the perfect excuse for doing good despite unworthiness.
1290) Jesus is the perfect excuse for pursuing good despite naysayers.
1291) Jesus is the perfect excuse for pursuing good despite mockers.
1292) Jesus is the perfect excuse for pursuing good despite scorners.
1293) Jesus is the perfect excuse for doing good despite sabotage.
1294) Jesus is the perfect excuse for doing good despite failure.
1295) Jesus is the perfect excuse for doing good despite yesterday.

1296) Yesterday is missing.
1297) Yesterday is missing in action.
1298) Where did yesterday go? Move forward.

1299) Stereotyping is a bad record.
1300) Stereotyping is not a fruit of the Spirit.
1301) Stereotyping is not forgiveness.
1302) Stereotyping has no faith in salvations choice.

1303) Stereotyping is not exercising salvations hope.

1304) Democrats support women who hate pro-life women.
1305) Democrats only like men who pretend to be women.
1306) Democrats love women as much as Democrats love fetus.
1307) Democrats only like women who support population control extremism.
1308) Democrats only like mothers who kill their own babies.
1309) Democrats would love to be rid of "Mother's Day".

1310) Happy "Mother's Day" Republicans.

1311) Outlaw Democrat's serial killing of human fetus.

1312) Christianity is the Religion of everlasting peace.
1313) Christianity is the Religion of human Creation.
1314) Christianity is the Religion evidencing one human race.
1315) Christianity is the Religion with a human History book.
1316) Christianity is the Religion with the only living God.
1317) Christianity is the Religion with the only resurrected God.
1318) Christianity is the Religion with the only forgiving God.
1319) Christianity is the Religion with the only ascended God.
1320) Christianity is the Religion with the only 33 years proven God.
1321) Christianity is the Religion with the only Heavenly God.
1322) Christianity is the Religion with the only God of hope.
1323) Christianity is the Religion with the only proven loving God.
1324) Christianity is the Religion with the only saving God.
1325) Christianity is the Religion with the only 2nd life evidenced God.
1326) Christianity is the only Religion with a God.

1327) A Religion without God is not a Religion.

1328) College degrees do not make you neighborly.
1329) College degrees do not make you forgiving.
1330) College degrees do not make you shun stereotyping.

1331) Be nonfiction.

1332) Reach for Christ beyond your worldly potential.

1333) Emotional IQ + instinctive IQ vary.

1334) Gender preservation preserves humanity.

1335) Gender destruction does not transform anything.
1336) Gender destruction creates an illusion.

1337) Fences keep dogs in and coyotes out.
1338) Fences make it easier to keep children from running into the street.
1339) Walls give people protection from creatures of the night.

1340) Discrimination is necessary - despise is not.

1341) Human Genesis was born from God.

1342) True compassion does not come from self-righteousness.
1343) True compassion does not come from a self-righteous dead end.
1344) True compassion does not come from only living once.

1345) Achieve completeness with Christ's golden key of salvation.

1346) Joyful not prideful.
1347) Contentment not pride.
1348) Happy not proud.

1349) True compassion warns about Hell.
1350) True compassion points to Christ's Heaven.
1351) True compassion discerns neighborly justice and opposes revenge.
1352) True compassion believes people are equally human from God.
1353) True compassion attempts tactful delivery of truth.

1354) If death is pardonable with reconciliation then so is crime.
1355) Support natural parenting goals.
1356) For children's sake - support natural marriage laws.

1357) A woman's womb is a human child's first room.

1358) We all came from Noah's Ark.
1359) We all came from Noah's family after the flood.

1360) Nations without God = Nations with extreme lack of wisdom.
1361) Nations without God = Nations with less discernment.
1362) Nations without God = Nations with less resistance to evil.
1363) Nations without God = Nations with less conscience.
1364) Nations without God = Nations with less truth.
1365) Nations without God = Nations with less regard for life.
1366) Nations without God = Nations without human equality defining.

1367) Property rights > money.
1368) Moral freedom > immoral freedom.

1369) Moral freedom sustains life.
1370) Moral freedom protects human life.
1371) Moral freedom protects business and property rights.
1372) Moral freedom seeks truth.
1373) Moral freedom opposes slavery.

1374) Immoral freedom accepts and legislates lies.
1375) Immoral freedom legislates destruction.
1376) Immoral freedom steals.
1377) Immoral freedom supports slavery.

1378) Christ is above Scientists.
1379) Christ is above Doctors.
1380) Christ is above Police.
1381) Christ is above mobs.
1382) Christ is above Congress.
1383) Christ is above Courts.
1384) Christ is above Judges.
1385) Christ is above the "Supreme Court."
1386) Christ is above Presidents.
1387) Christ is above unrepentant thieves & repentant murderers.
1388) Christ is above unrepentant murderers & repentant thieves.
1389) Christ is above Abortionists.
1390) Christ is above all false gods.
1391) Christ is above Christians.
1392) Christ is above Pastors.
1393) Christ is above Poets.
1394) Christ is above me.
1395) Christ is above New media.
1396) Christ is above liars.
1397) Christ is above evil conspirators.
1398) Christ is above Satan.
1399) Christ is above Mothers.
1400) Christ is above Fathers.
1401) Christ is above children.
1401) Christ is above animals.
1402) Christ is above the Bible.
1403) Christ is above death.
1404) Christ is equal with God.

1405) Christ is God with His Trinity.
1406) Christ is God with His Father.
1407) Christ is God with His Holy Spirit.
1408) Christ is Father God-Christ's-Spirit.
1409) Christ knows what everything means that we don't.
1410) Christ shows us humility versus pride.
1411) Christ gives mercy and reconciliation.
1412) Christ gives second chances.
1413) Christ is the second chance.
1414) Christ forgives with purpose.

1415) Forgiveness is ordered by God.
1416) Forgiveness is a key to loving neighbors rightly.

SECTION 8

1417) There is something between the lines.

1418) Love humans with Christ.
1419) Resist Satan
1420) Get close to God.

1421) PPTP = Proverbial, poetic truth pursuit.

1422) IWABW = I want a better World.
1423) IWABW with more of Christ.
1424) IWABW with more faith in Christ.
1425) IWABW with more peace in discussing evidence of God.
1426) IWABW with more freedom to discuss evidence of God.
1427) IWABW with more freedom to assess a risen, living God.
1428) IWABW with more freedom to assess God's Heavenly clues.
1429) IWABW with more freedom to discuss Christ's 2nd life clues.
1430) IWABW with more forgiveness, resolution & reconciliation.
1431) IWABW with less revenge & more Godly due process.
1432) IWABW with less revenge & more discernment.
1433) IWABW with less revenge & more neighborliness.
1434) IWABW with more "due process" under God.
1435) IWABW with more neighbors resolving without court.
1436) IWABW with more neighborly mercy under God.
1437) IWABW with more knowledge of equality from God.
1438) IWABW with more love for neighbor's property rights.
1439) IWABW with more reverence for God's love.

1440) IWABW with more love for TRUE Science under God.
1441) IWABW with more love for truth over lies.
1442) IWABW where lies against neighbors do not stand.
1443) IWABW where laws support natural parenthood.
1444) IWABW where laws support natural parent responsibility.
1445) IWABW where more children have their natural parents.
1446) IWABW where laws do not support government corruption.
1447) IWABW where laws do not support government kidnapping.
1448) IWABW where laws oppose creating orphans for Democrat slavery.
1449) IWABW where unrepentant baby killers are not called Doctors.
1450) IWABW where government cannot murder babies.
1451) IWABW where government is expected to view babies as human.
1452) IWABW where government is expected to view fetus as babies.
1453) IWABW where government is expected to outlaw abortion.
1454) IWABW where there is enforcement against killing baby fetus.
1455) IWABW that values dating for the purpose of natural marriage.
1456) IWABW that values God as Redeemer versus oppressor.
1457) IWABW that acknowledges Satan as the oppressor.
1458) IWABW that values natural laws as good awareness for youth.
1459) IWABW that values natures laws for children's natural protection.
1460) IWABW that values natures laws to promote natural instincts.
1461) IWABW that values all authorities being "under God."
1462) IWABW that values citizens as God's creation in His image.
1463) IWABW that values citizens as human neighbors.
1463) IWABW that values citizens as having wise rights from God.
1464) IWABW where authorities are honored but under God.
1465) IWABW where parents are honored but under God.
1466) IWABW where enemies are judged the same as neighbors.
1467) IWABW where Police protect God's ten commandments.
1468) IWABW where the physically ill have equal property rights.
1469) IWABW where most mentally ill have equal property rights.
1470) IWABW where medicinal consumers have equal property rights.
1471) IWABW where all medicines have safe, weakened regulated forms.
1472) IWABW where we are confident in 'law in order'.
1473) IWABW where we are cautious that 'over punishing is stealing.'
1474) IWABW where we remember for 'punishment to fit the crime.'
1475) IWABW where detainment for reconciliation > punishment.
1476) IWABW where detainment is done as necessity for safety.
1477) IWABW where detainment is lesser to punish & more for safety.
1478) IWABW where detainment rebukes messages of revenge.
1479) IWABW where detainment's clear goal is universal reconciling.
1480) IWABW where reconciliation systems rebuke money manipulations.
1481) IWABW where people understand the perils of unregulated

medicine.
1482) IWABW where people understand preference versus God's laws.
1483) IWABW where people understand freedom from others preferences.
1484) IWABW where people don't define pardonable sins as unpardonable.
1485) IWABW where people don't call things sins that are not sins.
1486) IWABW where there are fewer stigmas and people self-govern more.
1487) IWABW where avoiding unplanned pregnancy is the goal vs abortion.
1488) IWABW where women aren't having babies for Abortionists to harvest.
1489) IWABW where a proven 2nd life God is the basis for defining true religion.
1490) IWABW where fraudulent titles like "Planned Parenthood" are outlawed.
1491) IWABW where "Planned Parenthood" name is changed to "Planned Killing".
1492) IWABW where "Planned Killing" is outlawed.
1493) IWABW that seeks to be more like Heaven.
1494) IWABW that ponders how to be more like Christ's Holy Spirit.
1495) IWABW that studies Christ's commands to love God and people.
1496) IWABW that reconciles daily in keeping God's commandments.
1497) IWABW that makes it compelling to worship God in Spirit & truth.
1498) IWABW that is compelled enough to pray for a better World.
1499) IWABW remembering mortality and need for prayer.
1500) IWABW remembering human equality of "all have sinned" (Romans).
1501) IWABW recognizing women's menstrual cycles show equality.
1502) IWABW where obvious logic like 1+1 = 2 is still honored.
1503) IWABW where more people sing & others know when to stop.
1504) IWABW where repentance people are grateful for repentance.
1505) IWABW where repentance is recognized as a gift.
1506) IWABW where repentance is desired for a better path.
1507) IWABW where eternal pleasure is seen as good pleasure.
1508) IWABW that is passed down to future generations.
1509) IWABW that directs people to the best World in the 2nd life.
1510) IWABW with Godly Scientists making medicines not Evolutionists.
1511) IWABW with Godly Doctors in Hospitals not Evolutionists.
1512) IWABW with Godly Doctors in Hospitals not Scientologists.
1513) IWABW where Evolutionists are challenged to repent.
1514) IWABW where Evolutionists are awakened and wise up.

1515) IWABW where Evolutionists are seeing their fault & trusting Christ.
1516) IWABW where racists are shown God's forgiveness.
1517) IWABW where racists are prodded to trust Christ as God & Lord.
1518) IWABW where false accusers of racism are expected to repent.
1519) IWABW where false accusers of racism repent & trust Christ.
1520) IWABW with awareness of breaking physical addiction is 3 days.
1521) IWABW that knows medicine use is a choice not addiction.
1522) IWABW that knows dependency is not addiction.
1523) IWABW that knows people don't have to be caffeine dependent.
1524) IWABW that knows people are caffeine dependent by choice.
1525) IWABW that knows there are logical methods to end dependency.
1526) IWABW that knows what is healthy for the body, soul & mind.
1527) IWABW that desires a healthy body, soul & mind.
1528) IWABW that knows where the body, soul & mind come from.

1529) Stay in Christ's comfort zone.

1530) I am a Christian because I want to go to Heaven.
1531) I want the best life in Christ's Heaven.
1532) I am eternally optimistic in Christ.

1533) Christ's forgiveness would be worthless without resurrection.
1534) Christ still forgives because Christ rose from the dead.

1535) Planned mutilation is not planned parenthood.

1536) The Bible does not qualify stealing property from medicine
consumers.
1537) More diversity of personalities within moral realms not immoral.

1538) Silencing truth is the only way to ignore abortion as murder.

1539) Evolution's lie has bred systematic thievery through deception.

1540) Take care of your own house and nation.

1541) Dignity and mutual respect come from Biblical beliefs.

1542) Support death penalties for murderers not for baby fetus.

1543) I oppose the "Confederate Flag", which represents abolished
government.

1544) I oppose the "Confederate Flag", which represents a slave government.

1545) I support the "American Flag", which stands for racial equality from God.

1546) Every USA problem has always been less of Christ not more.

1547) Every positive USA solution uses Christ's reconciliation principles.

1548) I certainly have a distaste for some versus a full disliking or hating.

1549) I repent of frustration and anger that leads to hate.

1550) I renew a liking and loving realm by imagining God's view.

1551) Evolution will not grow wings in Hell.

1552) In Hell no one will evolve into growing wings.

1553) We can easily trace fossils & fish bones on land to Noah's flood.

1554) There are no fossils & fish bones on land millions of years old.

1555) We are equally human ancestors from Noah's Ark.

1556) God made land 'amidst the face of the deep". (Genesis 1)

1557) Were there any fish before God created the World?

1558) As I recall, God made the animals in His 7-day Creation.

1559) Part of Creation's process is explained in Genesis 1.

1560) I am locked into times cubicle & cannot explain everything.

1561) All human skin is a shade of brown from beige to dark brown.

1562) God is not colorblind he created all colors.

1563) We can live a better life with God's Spirit.

1564) We have solutions but we need God's Spirit to use them.

1565) We need to desire to have and use better World solutions.

1566) Microscopes have not been around long but eyes have.

1567) Use dung for fuel instead of food - Methanol over ethanol.

1568) Pray Christ's "Thy Kingdom come and will be done" anytime.

1560) Support Schools that teach God's laws of nature.

1561) Support Schools that teach Creations one race from God.

1562) Oppose Schools that teach against Creations one race.

1563) Oppose Schools that teach against natural laws.

1564) Support peace with Police.

1565) Reasonableness knows you need Police to detour chaos.

1566) Natural families have weaknesses but are not built on a lie.

1567) Christ was predestined to transform for people's clear choice.

1568) "Peace and Quiet" don't last long without a 2nd life.

1569) Pull time out of the box in Christ's eternal Spirit.
1570) Give up giving up by looking up and living up.

1571) Everyone deserves to be shown God's love.

1572) Christ showed, said & commanded loving everyone.

1573) Loving is not a simple easy feeling - God commanded it.

1574) Follow God's love and create good, positive feelings.

1575) Allow struggles to elevate you to solace time with God.

1576) Be a directional signal for Heaven & detour sign for Hell.

1577) Doesn't the light of Christ direct us to Heaven? Yes.

1578) Don't show your bad works, show your good works.

1579) All have bad & good works; good leads to good places.

1580) Don't deny bad works exist; confess to God vs. denying God.

1581) Temperance is a highly pursued fruit on success road.

1582) Honor God's gravity; we dissipate into oblivion without it.

1583) If we do not honor God's gravity we fall to our death.

1584) Honor God's eternal gravity in Christ.

1585) Godly encouragement is an infinite bank account.

1586) Monetary help is very limited, encouragement is not.

1587) True Christians should encourage in various ways more.

1588) Lasting love does not exist without The Bibles God.

1589) Life does not exist without Christ.

1590) Lasting hope does not exist without Christ.

1591) Nothing good lasts without Christ.
1592) Supernatural love is not blind.

1593) Supernatural love has the biggest vision in existence.

1594) Regard matters.

1595) If there is no regard then there is zero neighborliness.

1596) Wash your brain with living water.

1597) Lies hurt - truth helps.

1598) Death hurts - infinite truth supersedes.

1599) Lies bite - reality is a flashlight of truth.

1600) Invest in the greatest investment called Christ's Heaven.

SECTION 9:

1601) Forgiveness diffuses the power of lies.

1602) Dry ice hearts have no eternal blood flow.

1603) Satan is a tempter of evil - don't be that.

1604) The "Master Poet" is the Holy Spirit.

1605) God is real despite hypocrites.

1606) Emotionalism is a nutty god.

1607) Stereotyping positively is wrong too.

1608) God's Spirit & truth do not come separately.

1609) Good domino effects are better than bad ones.

1610) Never forget - over punishing is stealing.

1611) The death penalty for murder is not over punishing.

1612) Is there over punishing for murder? Yes.

1613) Torturing a murderer is not proper humane justice.

1614) Discernment adjudicating supports mercy against torture.

1615) Why have mercy on a torturer? Reconciliation. (Romans 3:23)

1616) I advocate death penalty for murder but not torture for torture.

1617) Am I 100% certain soft torture for torture is wrong? No, but God advocates mercy.

1618) What limit is there with torture justice before it is revenge?

1619) It is too difficult to measure justice in torture cases.

1620) I advocate the death penalty when torture results in death.

1621) I advocate solitary confinement for torture not resulting in death.
1622) I still support the death penalty and oppose torture.

1623) What about a medical procedure to remove an eye?

1624) There is no torture in a medical procedure.

1625) If someone removes another's eye in a crime - what is just?

1626) I would consider mercy or a medical procedure for justice.

1627) I would also ask the victim if they forgive & want mercy.

1628) I cannot confirm legalizing 'eye for eye' surgery justice.

1628) 'Eye for eye' surgery justice' is more sensible than torture.

1629) 'Eye for eye' 'surgery justice' is something I just thought of.

1630) 'Eye for eye' 'surgery justice' may or may not be good.

1631) 'Eye for eye' 'surgery justice' needs more ethical assessment.
1632) Is 'Eye for an eye surgery justice' my idea?
Not sure, just thought of it. (7/26/2020 – RHB)

1633) Be different not indifferent.

1634) I enjoy the fresh cooler weather feeling and fewer bugs.

1635) I enjoy the warmth & sauna type cleansing of warm weather.

1636) Do I qualify to speak? I have studied more Bible than Moses.

1637) Pride is a perverting spirit.

1638) Work for revival versus inconsiderately counting on the Rapture.

1639) Be a redeeming justice seeker.

1640) Doubting Christ is deathly boring.

1641) Recognize Democrats speech slavery methods.

1642) Should we build a double-wide wall at Canada's border?

1643) Americas Settlers were running from theocratic slavery.

1644) Human cultures are vain - Heavenly culture lasts.

1645) Christ show we need action not just words.

1646) Adopted sons of God = Sons of redeeming love.

1647) Oppose opposition to Christ and His laws.

1648) Set your goals so high that only God can see them clearly.

1649) Christ is the only one in History to permanently rise from death.

1650) Duh - God defeating death is why Christianity is popular.

1651) The 2nd life is less strange the more I view Christ's evidence.

1652) Democrat slavery today uses mobs & terror groups as their crackers.
1653) Anyone can kill but who can build up and maintain peace?

1654) Republican's love USA because it represents defeating slavery.

1655) Pay musicians for their performances.

1656) Music is a natural enjoyment of Creation.

1657) Music tuned properly rejoices with God.

1658) Be an infinite journey being.

1659) Do not die bored and hopeless with depraved destiny.

1660) Don't be a passing whim like those who laughed at Noah.

1661) Real wealth comes from investing in Christ's Heaven.

1662) Accepting life and deaths realities under God is humility.

1663) Our multi-faceted tricky minds need God's laws.

1664) Property rights come from God not memory tests.

1665) Do not steal redemption from people.

1666) Do not steal by over punishing.

1667) Jesus is real at all times not just in songs.

1668) Most Republicans don't lie because they believe in Hell.

1669) Abortionists calling pro-lifers racist is a 100% contradiction.

1670) Outlaw White abortionists from killing Black babies & visa-versa.

1671) Eventually, outlaw every abortion venue, if not now.

1672) Is White supremacy globalism what Democrats want?

1673) The Democrat who promotes killing babies is a true cracker.

1674) According to Democrats evolution beings have no intelligence.
1675) Humbly remember you are a sinner & discern your steps.

1676) Quality in life comes from revering its Creator.

1677) The irrational Democrats have always been known for mobs.

1678) Do not murder your own soul.

1679) People who pretend to believe in Christ land in Hell.

1680) People who trust their own goodness over God land in Hell.

1681) People who hate repenting to Christ land in Hell.

1682) Pro-murder and thieving are traits of the Hell bound.

1683) We are all Adamites & Noahmites = We are all Humanites.

1684) Blame God correctly.

1685) Loving evil desires destruction.

1686) Trust Hell's deniers to be dishonest.

1687) If you love medicine more than God, question your salvation.

1688) If we are not saved but think we are we land in Hell.

1689) If we are not saved but think we are we need salvation.

1690) If we are not saved but think we are, simply reassure.

1691) I suggest reaffirming salvation regularly because of us not God.

1692) I believe salvation is in stone if it was sincere.

1693) The mind is very tricky - question your own sincerity.

1694) The mind is very tricky - confirm your trust in Christ.

1695) If you really oppose slavery - oppose death.

1696) If you really oppose slavery - support resurrection.
1697) If you really oppose slavery - support 2nd life evidence.

1698) Reality = Democrats hate Republicans for outlawing slavery.

1699) Republicans outlawed slavery, in 1865.

1700) I am happy to be on freedom's side under God.

1701) I am happy to be on the side of pro-life freedom.

1702) I am happy to be in opposition to government murdering babies.

1703) Blame murderous hearts for abortion.

1704) The founding American Indians migrated from Noah's Ark too.

1705) Do not retire your mind.

1706) Job or no job - keep your mind in service.

1707) Make your mind be a vehicle of light in darkness.

1708) Do not be limited to being an "Earthling" - trust Christ.

1709) Trust the ascended "Supernatural Alien" named Jesus.

1710) Do not be a "Truthophobe".
1711) Do not be a "Christophobe".
1712) Do not be a "Heavenophobe".

1713) Be a "Hellophobe".

1714) "Christophobia" is the Hell of all phobias.

1715) Truth about lasting hope is good energy.

1716) Lies opposing lasting hope are negative energy.

1717) Discernment that balances reality is logical.

1718) True hope exists.

1719) A good future lasts forever.
1720) A good future requires unending hope.

1721) A good future requires finding unending hope.

1722) A good future requires trusting God's evidence of hope.

1723) A good future requires everlasting Christ as Lord.

1724) True hope valued inspires planning good successes.

1725) The Bible is only in proper context with Christ as the theme.

1726) Life breathes with forgiveness.

1727) Love people - compete with time.

1728) Awaken to life's renewing Spirit.
1729) Awaken with Christ at the end of earthly life.

1730) Democrats hate immigrants and love imposters.

1731) Christ's haters are not sane.

1732) My haters are not sane.

1733) No one needs to die for Jesus.

1734) Jesus can take care of Himself.

1735) If you have to die for faith in Jesus - keep that faith.
1736) It is okay to remove yourself from danger when standing for truth.
1737) It is okay to exercise self-defense when in danger for truth.
1738) It is okay to share truth strategically.
1739) It is okay to share truth strategically for efficiency.
1740) It is okay to share truth strategically for safety.
1741) It is okay to call Police for help when clearly threatened.

1742) Jesus died for us & wants us to live for Him not die.
1743) Jesus resurrected for us & wants us to die to greed & live redeemed.

1744) Mobs are Historically known for following hateful lies & distortion.

1745) Selfishness is natural and usually necessary.

1746) Greed is not necessary and is a sin.

1747) Selflessness for spiritual or heroic reason can be good.

1748) Our instincts know many intricate truths in this book.

1749) Our instincts recognize many details we often don't comply with.

1750) Our instinctive memory is huge.

1751) We often do not pay attention to numerous details our instincts brief.

1752) Be neighborly beyond Earth's norms.

1753) HTCR = How to cure racism.
1754) HTCR = believe people are equally created from God.
1755) HTCR = believe the risen Christ is God.
1756) HTCR = comply with Christ's neighbor loving commands.
1757) HTCR = rebuke false accusations of racism.
1758) HTCR = know the real definitions of racism.
1759) HTCR = know real racism believes in many gods.
1760) HTCR = know real racism rejects God.
1761) HTCR = regularly forgive and declare one race from God.
1762) HTCR = regularly share the Bible evidence of one race.
1763) HTCR = share that ethnicity came from language change.
1764) HTCR = cite that ethnicity doesn't matter - we are one race.
1765) HTCR = cite Religious differences matter not Ethnicity.
1766) HTCR = cite Christ is the only God against racism.
1767) HTCR = cite Christ proved His power over the flood.
1768) HTCR = cite we all came from Noah's family.
1769) HTCR = cite the flood disproves Evolution 100%.
1770) HTCR = cite Evolution represents real racism.
1771) HTCR = cite Evolution claims we are unequally evolved.
1772) HTCR = cite Evolution claiming we are animals.
1773) HTCR = cite Christ's resurrect proved Creation power.
1774) HTCR = cite Christ proved power to create Adam & Eve.
1775) HTCR = cite Christ tells us to "love our enemies".
1776) HTCR = cite forgiveness allows wisdom & discernment.
1777) HTCR = cite forgiveness is not for or against pardon.
1778) HTCR = cite mercy, fairness & discretion decided pardon.
1778) HTCR = cite discernment measures a neighborly resolve.
1779) HTCR = cite discernment measures safe justice for public.
1780) HTCR = cite reconciling need for nonracist majority.
1781) HTCR = cite reconciling law & order for peaceful majority.
1782) HTCR = cite "In God We Trust".
1783) HTCR = cite "One nation under God" means one equal race.
1784) HTCR = cite "The Declaration Of Independence" defines God.
1785) HTCR = cite "under God" means God the Creator.
1786) HTCR = cite God the Creator created one race from Adam.
1787) HTCR = cite we are all brown from beige to dark brown.
1788) HTCR = cite our differences are minor and our roots the same.
1789) HTCR = cite our similarities are far more than differences.
1790) HTCR = obvious evidences are worth sharing due to many lies.
1791) HTCR = share truth tactfully and strategically and move on.
1792) HTCR = pray for it, for eyes to be open, for apathetic to repent.

1793) PANW = Promote a neighborly World.
1794) CMM = Christ matters most.
1795) LAYHN = Love all your human neighbors.
1796) LAP = Love all people.
1796) CRWC = Cure racism with Christ.
1797) LAP WITH G-C-S = Love all people with God-Christ's-Spirit.

1798) America is not old Rome = We are built the opposite.
1799) America was built to have freedom to learn & share Christ.
1800) Prisons need to reflect Godly reconciliation instead of Rome.

SECTION 10:

1801) Goodness knows dignity from Christ's "Golden Rule".

1802) Goodness comes from Pro-life in Christ.

1803) Life is not a cliche'.
1804) Death is not a cliche'.
1805) The 2nd life is not a cliche'.
1806) Eternal life is not a cliche'.
1807) Hell is not a cliche'.
1808) Heaven is not a cliche'.
1809) Christ is not a cliche'.

1810) Natural marriage does not hate people who wish it were something else.

1811) Natural marriage represents where those who disagree came from.

1812) I can talk to anyone, anywhere and Christ still reigns.

1813) In "Go ye into all the World" Jesus eludes sharing with everyone.

1814) Social distance in God's breeze.

1815) Christ's first "how to" is to be saved from Hell.

1816) If you feel no urgency to warn of Hell - Question your salvation.

1817) God is against gluttony and for healthy diet.

1818) Potato chips are bad, but Potatoes healthy? Not exactly.

1819) Ever consider God's Spirit is the best psychoogist?

1820) The oldest religion is Christianity with Adam and Eve.

1821) Christianity was not named Christianity until after Christ.

1822) Yes, Judaism was Old Testament Christianity as I see it.

1823) The whole Bible represents Christianity & I call it that.

1824) White racists did not destroy ancient writings, God did.

1825) God destroyed ancient writings in Noah's flocd.

1826) Acts 11:26 = Disciples were 1st called Christian in Antioch.

1827) There is no Godly neighbor love in anti-Christ politics.

1828) Godly politics are the only politics that help people.

1829) Avidly discern Godly political theology.

1830) Headphones with only God's words would be ideal.

1831) God could give us His voice only if He wanted.

1832) God clearly wants us to hear variety and discern rightly.

1833) Has anyone noticed that Democrat leaders love lockdowns?

1834) My scope is different journeying vs. studying, but not my view.

1835) The people who say, "don't speak white boy" aren't racist?

1836) I am against being a slave to cliques.

1837) Those against love are beneath it, but love disagrees.

1838) The one who rose from the dead is my avenger.

1839) Scary movies where the monster won't die - neither will Jesus.

1840) Monster actors try stealing Christ's identity when they won't die.
1841) Jesus contains demons and puts them in the secured pit.

1842) Jesus is not a monster - He is loving God & cannot die.

1843) Killing black fetus is not racist according to Democrats.

1844) Democrats lynch via abortion today.
1845) Democrats lynch via tricking people into fighting over $10.
1846) Democrats lynch via tricking people into fighting period.
1847) Democrat media is like lynch mobs when they condone assault.

1848) The illusion that nothing Democrats do is racist is a world record setting lie.

1849) Opposing redemption for racists paints everything racist.

1850) Calling out true racism such as Evolution is good.

1851) Falsely accusing people of racism regularly is bad.

1852) Democrats use false racism accusations to bully people.
1853) Democrats use false racism accusations to trick people.
1854) Democrats never call out real racism like abortion or Evolution.

1855) Democrat leaders are serial killing abortionists.

1856) Republicans are taught to hate sin not people.

1857) Democrats promote hate for people and love sin.

1858) Caffeine users need to stop hating on nicotine users.
1859) Caffeine is probably more addictive than nicotine
1860) Caffeine users pick on nicotine because it is smoked.
1861) Nicotine can be used in gum or pill form, but it is dangerously strong in those forms versus burning out most nicotine when smoking.
1862) The healthier option is pills over smoking for the lungs, but you get more nicotine in pills which is a higher risk of stroke, because people get the whole 2 milligrams of nicotine in a lozenge.
1863) They make nicotine pills more expensive than smoking.
1864) I have heard cigarettes actually have glass particles.
1865) I promote abstinence from nicotine and caffeine; but various

strategies like decreasing dosages toward quitting if stopping at once doesn't last.

1866) I am not one who is disgusted with smokers.
1867) There are cigarette smokers with heavy withcrawals.
1868) Cigarette smoking costs more than caffeine products.
1869) I have seen cigarette smokers want money for more.
1870) I have not seen caffeine users want money for more.
1871) Know it only takes 3 days to break chemical withdrawal pains.
1872) If people test positive for caffeine should they lose their job?
1873) No, but that gives perspective to double standards.

1874) People should not worship drugs as a way to condemn.
1875) Drugs hurt the body, but hate and delusion kills the soul.

1876) Speak for Christ before finally being presentable at age120.
1877) Death is not a presentable place to speak for God.
1878) Death is not presentable but faith is and faith speaks.
1879) Faith speaks whether one's hair is presentable or not.

1880) A Christian's time is an anthem that never ends.
1881) Sing the Christian anthem of times endlessness.

1882) Hating baby murder is a good hate.
1883) Hating murder is a good hate.
1884) Hating the murderer is still not good.
1885) Seek humane justice that ends the killing.

1886) If you hate one person then you hate all people.
1887) If you hate one person then you hate God.
1888) Repenting of anger is your duty to God first.
1889) Repenting of anger is your duty to yourself.
1890) Repenting of anger is your duty for everyone.
1891) Living for hate results in Hell; repent for yourself.
1892) Trump haters are people haters and God haters.

1893) It is truly perverted to think baby killers are gcod politicians.

1894) Do not compete with me - compete with time against lies.

1895) President Trump is rightly selfish enough to help America.

1896) I have genuine excitement to be validated in Heaven.

1897) Remember that selfish is good, but greed is not.

1898) Children are not the devil.

1899) We are special enough not to know tomorrow.
1900) We are special enough to make today better than yesterday.
1901) We are special enough to have a choice of Heaven.

1902) Missing property is a snitch.
1903) Missing person's is a snitch.

1904) Love God's laws not man's laws.

1905) Two giants to kill = Racist evolution + legal abortion.

1906) Slavery is immoral and Democrats support immorality.

1907) A racist view makes everything racist = Democrats.

1908) Slavery can be defeated - Republicans defeated it!

1909) Loving Christ's reconciliation culture loves everyone.

1910) Extreme bigotry does not even know the Republican view.

1911) Live diligently in Heaven's direction.

1912) Peacemaking teaches the heart.
1913) A good Mother protects babies not aborts.
1914) A good Father protects babies not aborts.

1915) 2nd life curiosity is no reason to harm people.
1916) 2nd life curiosity is no reason to silence people.

1917) Humans do not evolve - they transform or die.

1918) Justice under God summarizes a peaceful eternity.

1919) Fraudulent religion has no God evidence of a 2nd life.

1920) Doctor your discernment with Heaven's chemistry.

1921) Anyone can please God with faith.

1922) Pure love - loves our Creator in return.

1923) Pretending politics are evil is Satan's ideal.

1924) Creativity styles oneself.
1925) Evolution will never be born.

1926) Black supremacy is equally as sinful as White supremacy.

1927) Take things one day at a time because that is all there is.

1928) Be a probiotic for Spirit and truth.

1929) Promoting disorder is not compassionate.

1930) Don't let Earthly culture stop you from choosing Heavenly culture.

1931) Today, you have succeeded beyond yesterday.

1932) G-C-S is the only perfect teacher.

1933) Christ created meditation.

1934) Pray for thieves to be obstructed.
1935) Pray for murderers to be obstructed.
1936) Pray for liars to be obstructed.

1937) Neither Blackness nor Whiteness can give a 2nd life.
1938) Blackness and Whiteness are false gods.

1939) Pain is a good enough clue of Hell for me.

1940) Focus on God's laws not on enemies.

1941) Natural laws guard against true racist infiltrations.

1942) Life does not continue without truth.

1943) A good nation is a Creation trusting nation.

1944) Truth matters more than this life.

1945) Lies are not civil.

1946) Can't find a husband? Blame Democrats for redefining.

1947) Democrats oppose spanking a child but kill them via abortion.

1948) Christ's Holy Spirit is my soul mate.

1949) Some false accusers of racism have racist motive.

1950) Be pro-Christ, pro-life, pro-husband and wife.

1951) Hide from pride - let God be your guide.

1952) Black & White people suck equally.
(Romans 3:23)

1953) Equality = "For all have sinned".
(Romans 3:23)

1954) Don't evolve - think!
1955) Don't evolve - work!
1956) Don't evolve - pray!
1957) Don't evolve - study!
1958) Don't evolve - forgive!
1959) Don't evolve - rest!
1960) Don't evolve - choose life!
1961) Don't evolve - choose Heaven!
1962) A Christian Republican President outlawed slavery.

1963) Abraham Lincoln outlawed slavery, in 1865.

1964) Israelite Moses married an Ethiopian woman.

1965) Fly with Christ.

1966) Seek wisdom versus results of haste.

1967) My haters see a miracle when I speak to them.

1968) Want with all your heart what can never be stolen.

1969) Christ is the greatest superhero of all time.

1970) 'Just say no' to dealing illegal drugs.

1971) Do not let losing deplore you - let choosing restore you.

1972) Use your brain for good.

1973) Good things lend toward life.

1974) More Christ - more redemption.

1975) More Christ - more comfort.

1976) More Christ - more truth.

1977) Seek Christ accreditation most.

1978) Christian meditation is superior to other meditation.

1979) Matter does not matter much without energy.

1980) Truth should be one of our most protected resources.

1981) Hope people get tired of this psychotic World & desire Heaven.

1982) Christianity is an everlasting life class.

1983) Politics should support life.
1984) Politics are supposed to be about supporting life.

1985) There is one conversion = death's road to life's road.

1986) Houses are not show pieces - they are for living.

1987) Sin's consent obstructs successes joys.

1988) Lift your head toward Heaven and bow your heart.

1989) There are many ways to pray to Christ.

1990) Pray while walking, kneeling, singing privately or publicly.

1991) Babies love women - abortion does not.

1992) Plan to live 120 years - prioritize like today is your last.

1993) Diligence takes time.

1994) Diligence needs time, and respected space from others.

1995) You will not evolve into a butterfly in Hell.

1996) Live with the acceptance of human limitations.

1997) I am an "Eternalist", and that is my visionary perspective.

1998) I believe in international independence with coalitions.

1999) I believe in promoting independence under God globally.

2000) I believe I should manage well, and my neighbors can too.

SECTION 11:

2001) Hell being around the bend drives me to share Christ.
2002) There is plenty of Heaven to go around.
2003) I lose nothing in Heaven by inviting more people.
2004) I actually gain rewards in Heaven for inviting people.
2005) No one I invite to Heaven will steal from me there.
2006) No one I invite to Heaven will steal from anyone there.
2007) Heaven, Hell and death drive me to share Heaven.
2008) Sharing Heavens choice is truly good.
2009) Defining good is not easy; Heaven is clearly good.
2010) Having Heavens promise inspires me to share goodness.
2011) Heaven is one of few things I know is 100% good.
2012) The only way to Heaven is to have a 2nd life.
2013) The only evidence of Heaven is resurrected Christ.
2014) Christ showed 100% goodness like Heaven's hope.

Romans 10:9 = "If you will share with your voice that Jesus is Lord and believe in your heart that God has raised Him from the dead, you will be saved."

John 3:17 = "For God sent not His Son into the World to condemn the World but that the World through Him might be saved."

2015) All ethnicities have melanin in their skin.

2016) When sin is digging your grave confess & be redeemed.

2017) Reject outer body experiences of looking down on yourself.

2018) Give God's energy to people.

2019) Share God's pure oxygen of truth and Spirit.

2020) Spirits and winds are not visible but their expression is.

2021) We love silence until the volume of boredom rises.

2022) Celebrate the Holy Ghost especially in October.

2023) Everything eventually brings praise to God.

2024) Do not have a clique affinity for outfits of illusion.

2025) People hide in cliques from realities observations.

2026) After you wake up follow dreams not nightmares.

2027) The infinity of a good normal is only lived in Heaven.

2028) I ponder life's vanity when I watch old shows with dead casts.

2029) I travel a lot from thought to thought and observation.

2030) I celebrate real Ghosts in October NOT fake = Christ's Ghost.

2031) I often run from luck not knowing if it is good or bad.

2032) Rise beyond limited oppressive vision onto 'Prayer Mountain'.

2033) Oppressiveness from a political class or God?

2034) Promote nations under God not under oppression.

2035) There will always be some oppression on earth.

2036) Despite oppression on earth don't let it reign in theory or heart.

2037) "One nation under God" versus giving up against oppressors.

2038) "Under God" keeps us in the battle of truth.

2039) Throwing out the battle of truth gives way to physical battles.

2040) The battle of truth allows us to keep a purging system versus war.

2041) Stay in the peace leaning battle of truth "under God".

2042) I never met a level headed person, mostly round.

2043) Pride often renders the educated as primitive.

2044) A woman's womb is not a death chamber.

2045) View humans as unique spiritual beings.

2046) Should I view people through God's lens or mine?
2047) I can't exactly view people through God's lens.
2048) View people through God's forgiveness and laws.
2049) View people as you view yourself.
2050) View people as independent managers.
2051) View people as deserving of Christ's reconciliation principles.
2052) View people as deserving of freedom and independence.
2053) View people as deserving property rights.
2054) View people as deserving the right to life.
2055) View people as having good days and bad days.
2056) View people as independent but needing help sometimes.
2057) View people as imperfect and needing God's wisdom.
2058) View people as created equally in God's image.
2059) View people as loved and desired by Christ.
2060) View people as needing to understand the 2nd life.
2061) View people as victims of worldly lies.
2062) View people as journeymen who need a basic map.
2063) View people as energetically inconsistent.
2064) View people as wanting a laugh at times.
2065) View people as wanting a periodic emotional boost.
2066) View people primarily as spiritual beings.
2067) View people as mostly needing spiritual purpose.
2068) View yourself as mostly needing spiritual purpose.
2069) View yourself as in need of God's guidance 24/7.

2070) People manage themselves but periodic truth shared is good.
2071) People have 2 differences = loving God or not.
2072) Clarity of understanding God varies.
2073) Clarity of how to follow God varies.
2074) Some people are overly picky versus relying on faith.
2075) Some people mix personal preferences with God's law.
2076) Some people hate God and will not relate.
2077) Some people claim God and hate to hear his name.
2078) I speak to the heart, because life is busy.
2079) I speak to the heart, because schedules lack time.
2080) I speak to the heart, because the mind is busy.
2081) I speak now, because when else can we?
2082) I speak now, because relevant times come.
2083) I speak now about God, BUT He is always relevant.
2084) Don't be too busy to remember God.

2085) God is like the water in your body = Always relevant.

2086) A woman's womb is not a slaughterhouse.
2087) A woman's womb is an ordained giver of life.
2088) A woman's womb is an ordained nurturer of life.

2089) Dirt does not need money - how is it poor?
2090) Does dirt even need grass?
2091) Dirt helps grow things if it has water.
2092) Does dirt need water if it is not growing anything?
2093) Where does dirt get its value?
2094) God created dirt. (Genesis 1)
2095) Dirt is what we walk on.
2096) Dirt does not have financial problems.
2097) Dirt just does what God tells it.
2098) Dirt protects seeds and holds water for them.
2099) Dirt protects roots.
2100) The Bible says we are made from dirt.
2101) Is our main job to protect seeds of truth?
2102) Is our main job to protect roots of truth?
2103) Is our main job to absorb the minerals?
2104) Debt represents being poorer than dirt.
2105) Without debt we function like dirt but do more.
2106) We function like dirt by protecting truth seeds.
2107) We function like dirt by protecting truth rights.
2108) Dirt cannot be seed planters, but we can.
2109) Dirt does not worry about debt; we shouldn't either.

2110) No need to worry but we will some, work on it.

2111) I prefer to be judged by God now than later.
2112) I go to God's court every day with no delays.
2113) God gives us a prayer option "forgiveness court".
2114) I prefer God's "forgiveness court" over the "too late court".

2115) Pray for America to value God instead of oppressor regimes.

2116) Feel confident in planting truth seeds no matter the result.
2118) The ground deals with God after the seeds are planted.
2119) Some ground is fertile and some ground is not.
2120) Sower's plant, the ground receives and God grows.
2121) Sowers need to make sure seeds have some water.
2122) God provides some water for seeds.
2123) God created the pro-creation process of natural growth.

2124) Choosing a Godly marriage partner matters.

2125) Everyone has equal opportunity to choose Christ's Heaven.
2126) Everyone has equal opportunity to pursue wisdom.
2127) Everyone has equal rights to receive Christ's forgiveness.

2128) Strive to maintain Spirit awareness when busy or not.
2129) Strive to maintain Spirit awareness in quiet or noise.

2130) Gratitude for property understands "thou shalt not steal".

2131) When the eyes get sleepy the body follows.

2132) True justice has a Godly blueprint.

2133) Individuals behaving better makes a nation better.

2134) Keep the feet of your soul on redemptions path.

2135) Heaven's path or redemptions? Redemption brings Heaven.

2136) We don't go to Heaven without redemption.

2137) Put your soul's feet on redemptions path from Heaven.

2138) Trust Christ's redemption for "Heavens Hope Road".

2139) "Prayer Mountain" asks God for visionary understanding.
2140) "Prayer Mountain" asks God for wisdom and patience.
2141) "Prayer Mountain" asks God for redeeming strength.
2142) "Prayer Mountain" asks God for 365 days of intercession.
2143) Loving people is often not easy it is a command from God.

2144) One of the biggest lies = Politics are offensive.
2145) "Thou shalt not kill" is not offensive, killing is.
2146) "Thou shalt not steal" is not offensive, stealing is.

2147) Truth disrespects lie's.

2148) Black Republican lives matter.
2149) Black Republicans have pro-life positive value.
2150) Black Christian lives matter.
2151) Black Muslim lives need to repent for resurrection.
2152) White Christian lives matter.
2153) White Muslim lives need to repent for resurrection.

2154) The King of Black freedom from slavery = Abraham Lincoln.
2155) Republicans freed the most African slaves in History.
(My estimate = Lincoln, 1865 + George W. Bush helping free Angola, AF.)

2156) Black people didn't end slavery; a White majority did.
2157) White Republicans ended slavery; White Democrats opposed.
2158) Yes, Black people helped fight the war on both sides.
2159) The White population was far bigger than the Black population.
2160) A large White population opposed many Whites to end slavery.
2161) Once again, I say, "yes, Black people helped fight on both sides".

2162) Serial killing of fetus should not be legal.

2163) Trust that doesn't work isn't really trust.
(James 2:26 - "Faith without works is dead.")

2164) Anyone who thinks Trump is racist is delusional or lying.

2165) Many who think Republicans are racist are delusional or lying.

2166) Peaceable living takes peaceable understanding.

2167) Islamic cults chopping off heads is NOT peaceful.

2168) Christianity is the religion of lasting peace, not a cult.

2169) Democrat medias repetitive lies radicalize & create killers.

2170) Worshiping people as objects does not get them to Heaven.
2171) The way to awaken people is rebuking illusions for truth.
2172) People may or may not wise up, but truth is the way to awaken.

2173) Be wise like "In God We Trust" Republicans who mean it.

2174) Say "no" to laws against God's commandments.
2175) Say "no" to Democrats murderous abortion.
2176) Say "no" to Democrats "Planned Population Control".
2177) Say "no" to "Planned Parenthood's" fraudulent name.
2178) Say "no" to lies being legislated into law.

2179) Democrats welcome thieves to steal legal migrants place in line.

2180) Salvation's cost is not payable by man common man.
2181) Salvation's cost is out of this World.
2182) Salvation's cost is supernatural.
2183) Salvation's cost has already been paid for.
2184) Salvation's cost is free for you and me.

2185) True racism comes from many places.
2186) Racism comes from new age cults.
2187) Racism comes from false religions rejecting Christ.
2188) Racism comes from evolution beliefs.
2189) Racism comes from atheism.
2190) Racism comes from fake Christians.
2191) Racism comes from ancestral worship.
2192) Racism comes from many things NOT the living God.

2193) A fetus is a living baby already named by God.
2194) A fetus has an umbilical cord for oxygen and food.
2195) Many name their fetus and sing him or her songs.
2196) Many people laugh and talk to their fetus.
2197) The fetus takes on the last name of parents.
2198) The fetus is often named after the Father or Mother.
2199) Safety is intricately followed to care of the fetus.
2200) Loving people are careful not to fall while pregnant.
2201) It is natural and rational to eat healthy while pregnant.

SECTION 12:

2202) Black and White Republicans like freedom.
2203) Black and White Democrats oppose freedom.

2204) There is no greater freedom than rising with Christ.
1 Thessalonians 4:16 = "The dead in Christ shall rise first."

2205) Killing a human fetus is not bigotry against children?
2206) Who wants to be bothered with children? Not Abortionists.
2207) Government wanting to kill your fetus is not bigotry?

2208) Homeless children increase was a direct result of LBGTQ laws.
2209) Homeless children increase was a direct result of illegal border
crossing.

2210) Believing multiple Democrat lies leads many to schizophrenia.

2211) Write 1,000 times, "The Democrats are the Party of slavery".

2212) Rejecting resurrections creation power is real racism.
2213) If you hate the Creator you hate the human race.

2214) USA serial killers running to Mexico from American Police is not real
immigration.
2215) Laws against nature render your life as irrelevant.
2216) Laws against nature elude that no one matters.
2217) Laws against nature elude that God does not matter.
2218) Laws against nature elude that reality does not matter.
2219) Laws against nature only give power to the biggest bully.

2220) Laws of God give property rights to everyone.
2221) Laws of God define us as equally human.
2222) Laws of God view government under God like everyone else.
2223) Laws of God enforce against bullies stealing from others.
2224) Laws of God give the right to life.
2225) Laws of God protect children.
2226) Laws of God expect natural parent responsibility.
2227) Laws of God oppose lying to about others.

2228) You are not sharing holy love if you are not sharing Christ.

2229) Defund Evolution in schools.
2230) Teaching Evolution in schools is clear systematic racism.

2231) You clearly want Hell if you don't want Christ's fruit.

2232) No matter what people say or do - trust Christ's forgiveness.

2233) Medicinal abstinence is a false gospel, but a wise & healthy goal.

2234) A sound (rational) mind is also a sober mind.

2235) Love = "Thou shalt not murder".
2236) Love = "Thou shalt not steal".
2237) Love = "Thou shalt not covet".
2238) Love = "Thou shalt not commit adultery".
2239) Love = "Revering the Sabbath".
2240) Love = "Revering Creations God in Christ".
2241) Love = "Honoring Father and Mother".
2242) Love = "Loving your neighbor as yourself".
2243) Love = "Not lying about neighbors".
2244) Love = Loving truth not loving lies.
2245) Love = "Keeping God's commandments".
2246) Love = "Delighting in the laws of God daily".
2247) Love = Granting reconciliation to neighbors.
2248) Love = Granting redemption to neighbors.
2249) Love = Rebuking lies with mercy and truth.
2250) Love = Expecting peacemaking but is patient.
2251) Love = Shares Christ's salvation message.
2252) Love = Prays for enemies.
2253) Love = Forgives friends and enemies.
2254) Love = Forgives self.
2255) Love = Accepts Christ's forgiveness.
2256) Love = Accepts and trusts Christ's salvation.

2257) Equality = Romans 3:23
2258) Equal opportunity = Romans 6:23

2259) Evolution = Animalistic Inequality.
2260) Creation = Human equality under God.

2261) Forgiveness is one of the most obvious evidences of God.

2262) Christ teaches daily forgiveness in His "Lord's Prayer".

2263) Matthew 6:9-13 = The Lord's Prayer.

2264) Mark 11:25-26 = Forgive sins or God won't forgive yours.

2265) Christ saved the believing thief on the cross beside him.
2266) The trusting thief beside Jesus was saved just before death.

2267) Unforgiveness is a spirit of Hell.
2268) A spirit of Hell already exists in many people.

2269) Fear Hell's warming far more than Global warming.

2270) Faith is not always good.
2271) Faith in death & lies are not good faiths.

2272) Extremism = Investing in lies + rejecting life's realities.

2273) What loves you - truth or lies? Truth.

2274) Creations words say – love, share, pray and live.

2275) The truth of death is painful.
2276) The truth of life is relieving.

2277) Forgiveness is accompanied by understanding.
(Luke 23)
2278) Be a loving parent not a proud parent.

2279) If you see me dreaming of Heaven, let me dream.
2280) If you see me dreaming of Heaven, join me.

2281) Jesus = The Great Reviver.

2282) The greatest teacher of all time said the "Golden Rule".
2283) Luke 6:31, "Do to others as you would have them do to you."

2284) Embrace Jesus and His values in all parts of society.
2285) Politics are a part of society.
2286) Politics and governing have neighbors in them.
2287) Politics have enemies in them.
2288) Politics decide whether we follow Godly laws or not.

2289) Laws are like a road map.
2290) Road maps for Satan should be contested.
2291) Road maps to Hell should be obstructed.
2292) Road maps for parentless chaos should be obstructed.
2293) Use road maps of God's neighborly laws.
2294) Promote road maps of God's laws in politics.
2295) Promote human equality under God in politics.

2296) Life without God's guidance is no good.
2297) Life without God revered in governing is not neighborly.

2298) How a mind hears of Christ & is mean spirited is baffling.

2299) Chase the dime and you will run out of time.
2300) Embrace God's grace, and you will always have space.
2301) Follow God's love, and your soul soar's like a dove.

2302) Turn from people not from God.

2303) Learn to see yourself as God wants you to.
2304) Learn to see others as God wants you to.

2305) A nation without God = A nation without redemption.
2306) A nation without God = A nation without pure love.
2307) A nation without God = A nation without forgiveness.
2308) A nation without God = A nation without wisdom.
2309) A nation without God = A nation without humility.
2310) A nation without God = A nation without truth value.
2311) A nation without God = A nation without preeminent truth.
2312) A nation without God = A nation without human equality.

2313) Choose resurrection = Resurrection emphasis culture.

2314) There are many teachers but only one eternal Savior.

2315) 2 ultimate things exist = Pro-Christ people & Anti-Christ people.

2316) Do not replace forgiveness under just law with corrupt law
tolerance.

2317) God's love does not reject an unborn baby.

2318) True racism is a sin; it is a rejection of Creation equality.

2319) The only good ways to make money are neighbor loving ways.

2320) No green light for murdering unborn babies.

2321) Instead of mutilating unborn babies do a C-section.

2322) A leader for mutilating the unborn is not a good leader.

2323) How can one love an unborn good thought if they love abortion?

2324) Start thinking about what is good in God's eyes.

2325) Racism is a rejection of God the Creator.

2326) False racism accusers also promote 3rd gender illusion.

2327) Perversion of law + real law = No law = Tyranny.

2328) Stop being receptive to obvious Satanic messages.

2329) Truth is superior to lies of racist Evolution.
2330) Truth is superior to lies of pro-abortion being good.
2331) Truth is superior to same sex parenting being taught.
2332) Truth is superior to ignorance of pain and Hell.
2333) Truth is superior to faking racism while opposing God.
2334) Truth is superior to death.

2335) Jesus is Lord over the Old and New Testaments.

2336) Attempting to leave God out of the future is bad politics.

2337) Life is a sanctuary to those who value it.

2338) Outer peace can be stolen, but Christ's inner peace cannot.

2339) Do not be an alien to Christ's universe of lasting love.

2340) How much should people honor parents? As God pleasers.
(Ephesians 6:5-6)

2341) Stars do not shine in Hell.

2342) God created natural sex for marriage.
2343) Jesus did not kill those who disrespected Him, but Hell is coming.

2344) God's resurrection power is revealed every time we wake up.

2345) Closer to God = further from racism.

2346) Love Hell's warning, and embrace Heaven's peace.

2347) Solve problems by avoiding them; promote God's neighborly laws.

2348) Wash your brain with pure everlasting love.

2349) Teaching evolution has increased real racism cross culturally.

2350) Do not evolve - think.

2351) Everyone can repent in Christ whether racist or not.

2352) Save the nation with Christ's ways.
(Matthew 22:36-40; Matthew 5-7)

2353) Men and women are equally human under God.

2354) Christophobia is strange since He offers Earth time forgiveness.
2355) Christophobia is not strange when He sends rejecters to Hell.

2356) Hell is for haters of the God's Son of Heaven.
2357) Hell is for haters of Christ proving resurrections way to Heaven.

2358) Freedom under God = love of life.
2359) Freedom under God haters = love of chain links.

2360) Non-Christians are not spiritual children of God.
2361) Non-Christians are physical children of God.

2362) Racists do not even have pure love for their own family or self.

2363) When it comes to sense - every thought counts.

2364) 'Rolls Royce' is nothing compared to the vehicle to Heaven in
Christ.

2365) It is neither crazy nor extreme to stand for protecting babies.

2366) True greatness lives forever in grace by God's great power.

2367) Do not tolerate murder and stealing - forgive it, reconciled it.

2368) God's way is not that complicated - people are.

2369) We all deserve to be loved, Christ commanded it & showed it.

2370) Love your soul more than your sin.
2371) Love your soul more than your skin.
2372) Love your soul more than your kin.
2373) Love your soul more than your twin.

2374) Legislate truthful definitions into law.

2375) You cannot count into infinity without #1.

2376) Open borders is what American Indians had.

2377) Repentant sinner's superhero = Jesus Christ.

2378) Quit quitting on life's knitting thread of no ending.

2379) What are the most important political issues?
2380) We are equally human created in God's image.
2381) We are equally human under God.
2382) God tells humans to follow the "Golden Rule".
2383) Authorities are equally human, "Golden Rule".
2384) Be pro-life in everything = "thou shalt not murder".
2385) Have pro-husband and wife laws for children's sake.
2386) Have pro-husband and wife laws for humanity's remembrance.
2387) Have pro-husband and wife laws for God's remembrance.
2388) Honor God's ten neighborly commandments.
2389) Honor Christ's laws of reconciliation and forgiveness with mercy.

2390) God dwells in the light of hope.
2391) God turns the lights down on us daily.
2392) God turns the lights on for us daily.
2393) God gives us the awareness of His light daily.
2394) God gives us the choice of His Heavenly hope daily.
2395) Recognize God's hope, be wise, and trust Christ as Lord.

SECTION 13:

2396) I am not attracted to people who think nearly everyone is ugly.
2397) Thinking nearly everyone is ugly comes from an ugly heart.

2398) What does it feel like to be the most hated?
2399) I didn't know I won the most hated trophy.
2400) I figure haters of people hate on everyone the same way.
2401) Hate sin - love people - is God's command.

2402) Opposing false racism claims does not get you out of Hell.

2403) Democrat slavery today uses mobs as their crackers.

2404) Democrats hate women as much as they hate fetus.

2405) Democrats favorite color is to hate any color in various ways.

2406) All human lives matter equally from God is the right philosophy.

2407) We need more jail for people who assault against "All Lives Matter".

2408) B.L.A.M. = Black, blue and all lives matter. In Christ we trust.

2409) People who hate Police are for more violence not less.

2410) Facts over oppression and lies.
2411) We want orderly Police under God not irrational mobs.

2412) Americans want the freedom to shop without mob assaults.

2413) Americans want the freedom to drive without mob assaults.

2414) Democrats loves silencing truth and disagreements.

2415) American drug cartel doesn't exist just like Black racism doesn't?

2416) American Police try to do better - their haters do not.

2417) Ben Carson's life matters.

2418) I oppose throwing America into the dumpster.

2419) America is a rational nation, except for the Democrat half.

2420) Lies are irrational.
2421) Threats of violent assault are irrational.
2422) Violent assaults are irrational.
2423) Revenge is irrational.

2424) Stop neighborhood violence & there is less Police presence.

2425) I avoid Police mostly + support Police.

2426) Democrats mobs bullying people is not attempted slavery?

2427) An error is not a lie.
2428) Stats change & it is a lie to compare last week's stat to this week
and claim someone who quoted last week's last week is lying on old tape
while not citing the truth that it was said last week (media did that to
Trump).

2429) Democrats have routine lies about life's roots.
2430) How do Democrat media lies help you long term?
2431) How do Democrat leaders lies help you long term?
2432) How do Democrat medias thieving promotions help your future?
2433) How do Democrat leaders thieving promotions help your future?

2434) Democrats "no lives matter" groups are not well disguised.

2435) America was great before crack cocaine, in the 1980's.
2436) America was great before legalized abortion, in 1973.
2437) America was great before media started promoting assaults.
2438) America was great before same sex marriage under Obama.
2439) At least half America still supports working toward excellence.
2440) Wise people know God's greatness commands neighborly laws.

2441) We are locked into times cubicle with Heavens open door.
2442) When earth time ends, Heaven's door will be closed.
2443) Enter into Christ while you are still in times cubicle.

2444) Democrat diversity does not even like a human fetus.

2445) Let Police keep detouring cartels from stealing people's property.

2446) Rejection can hurt because it can ruin plans and hopes.

2447) God's Spirit is not one tone; He has many + atonal in tune.
2448) God's Spirit is the comforting power with everlasting energy.

2449) Jewish Jesus was a shade of brown because all people are.
2450) So what if Jesus was tanner or not; He represents all humanity.
2451) Jesus represents all humanity from Adam.
2452) Jesus represents being the 2nd Adam for the 2nd life.

2453) John Quincy Adams was the key to ending slavery.
2454) Abraham Lincoln was the "Commander and Chief" who ended slavery.

2455) I believe that black lives matter, but I don't condone Marxism.
2456) I believe that black lives matter, but I don't condone Islam.
2457) I believe that black lives matter, but I don't condone abortion.
2458) I believe that black lives matter, but I don't condone cartels.
2459) I believe that black lives matter, but I don't condone cliques.
2460) I believe that black lives matter, but I don't hate Police.
2461) I believe that black lives matter, and I believe all lives matter.
2462) I believe that black lives matter, but I oppose irrational mobs.
2463) I believe that black lives matter, but I oppose irrational thinking.
2464) I believe that black lives matter, but I oppose stealing.
2465) I believe that black lives matter, but I oppose assault.
2466) I believe that black lives matter, and that white lives matter too.
2467) I believe that black lives matter to Christ not to Democrats.

2468) The hopelessness of death is overcome in trusting Christ.
2469) Run times race of truth over lies for Christ's sake & souls.

2470) Make killing American fetus a hate crime against babies.

2471) Republicans expect the whole World not to be racist.
2472) The largest non-racist group in History is American Republicans.
2473) Republicans expecting Black people not to be racist is equality.
2474) Why expect only Republicans not to be racist? Expect no one to.
2475) You are falsely called racist unless obeying Democrat slave masters.
2476) Black racism is just as ugly as white racism.
2477) Equally opposing black and white supremacy is neighborly not racist.
2478) White Democrats use black Democrats to define racism as white only.

2478) God created one race and we are all equally sinners.
2479) Democrats hate Christ because He judges black & white equally.
2480) Support God's one race theology and forgive regardless of results.

2481) Democrats teach that God's ten neighborly commands are racist.
2482) God's laws are to protect every one of all ethnicities from theft.
2483) God's laws are to protect all ethnicities from murder.
2484) God's laws protect every nation who reveres His laws.
2485) God's laws will not be 100% enforced to save lives until Heaven.
2486) We can do better to enforce God's life & property protection rights.
2487) Step 1 to improving property & life protection is revering God.
2488) Step 2 for improving protection of people is revering God's laws.

2489) If we say we revere God but not His laws - we don't trust God.

2490) Republicans are the World champions against slavery.
2491) Republicans are the World champions against racism.
2492) Republicans have been the champions against slavery 160 years.

2493) When have you heard a Democrat be against cartel slavery?
2494) When have you heard a Democrat be against Islamic slave trade?
2495) When have you heard a Democrat be against fake marriage
adoption?

2496) Only Democrats half of America have been substantially ill-willed
throughout its History.

2497) Jesus lived here 33 years and Allah 0 = Mocking Christians is
senseless.

2498) Do not be like the OCD legalist / Pharisee.

2499) If they resisted/fought Police we aren't interested in media narrative.
2500) If someone fought Police and got hurt - it is their own fault.
2501) If someone fought Police and got hurt - it is for courts not mobs.
2502) If someone fought Police and got hurt - it is for courts not media.

2503) Democrats represent the true racist, slave master thieves.
2504) Slave masters are thieves, and Democrats promote thieving.
2505) Racism is steals peace by lies and delusions about humanity.

2506) Is "Planned Parenthood" run by the old KKK?
2507) Is population control extremism run by the old KKK?

2508) Are LBGTQ activists for population extremism run by the KKK?
2509) Are Antifa terrorists a mixture of all the above?
2510) Are Antifa terrorists international? Yes.
2511) KKK hated Jews and so do Islamic cults and Nazi's.
2512) KKK and Nazi's with Nazi tattoos work together a lot.
2513) Antifa and Democrat mobs support Islam & oppose Christ.
2514) All of the above support's abortion.
2515) All of the above support's fraudulent "Planned Parenthood".
2516) All of the above support's oppressive Global regimes.
2517) All of the above support's Global supremacy government.
2518) They all oppose life and property rights.
2519) They pretend to care about certain lives while opposing life rights.

2520) God cares - Democrat groups don't!

2521) Repent daily.

Proverbs 8:17 = "I love them that love me, and those that seek me early shall find me."

2522) Personal preferences help you cope with life.
2523) Personal preferences are not laws for everyone = They are preferences.
2524) Work to distinguish between God's basic governing laws and preferences.

2526) Support yourself with resurrected Christ's eternal life insurance.

2527) Falsely accusing of racism to gratify your own doesn't oppose racism.

2528) Sane people doubly support Police after Democrat's mob mayhems.

2529) If your life matters to me I point you to Christianity not Islam.

2530) Islamic cult regimes are behind the Antifa / BLM mob mayhem.

2531) Islamic cult regimes are supporting the Marxism.

2532) When Christ matters to you then Life matters to you.

2533) Everyone is a natural born racist; trusting Christ is the only cure.

2534) There is no such thing as a true Christian racist.
2535) If someone is a racist then they are not a true Christian.
2536) The Christian soul knows what the mind does not.
2537) A new Christian may not know the definitions yet.

2538) I am not colorblind or assault blind: assault is assault.

2539) I am for legalizing 2% prescription pill forms of all medicine.

2540) A person can even find Christ by hearing His haters and opposing.

2541) Democrat media prefer a Black Police die versus a Black murderer.

2542) Only Christ has the heart cure for racism.
2543) Anger management is a mind and heart battle.
2544) Anger mismanagement occurs for many reasons.
2545) Racist bigotry is only 1 of many reasons anger is mismanaged.

2545) If someone is truly racist that is their choice of Hell over Heaven.
2546) If someone is truly racist that is their choice.
2547) We cannot enforce against racism only assault, theft & defamation.

2548) Dream so big that you find Jesus as Lord.

2549) Angry hate is not truth it is emotion.

2550) Black women aren't beautiful when they oppose Democrats?
2551) Democrats like to pimp Black women.

2552) Africa started slavery not America.
2553) Is it fair to portray Africa as a slave nation or just the guilty?
2554) Some of Africa still has Islamic slave trade today.

2555) Living for lies gets you nowhere but to chaotic Hell.

2556) Jesus is the record standard of evidence of God.
2557) No one has risen above Christ's standard of proof for God.
2558) No one has even come close to Christ's standard of proof for God.

2559) Christianity ruled the World on Noah's Ark.
2560) Christianity will rule Heaven and Earth 100% after this World.

2561) Pray for wisdom, understanding and awareness to apply truth.
2562) Remember theology in various settings.

2563) Don't wait to grow wrinkles before being comfortable in your skin.

2564) Real bigotry sees me without knowing the facts and is already angry.

2565) Corrupt media has field days of lies while people are busy working.

2566) Know that stomachs will love God's laws if the hearts do not.

2567) "No Trespassing" is something Democrat leaders don't understand.

2568) Using logic is not racist it is a rejection of racist evolution.

2569) The mind is built to use logic not to stay idle for evolving.

2570) Corrupt news puts America last.

2571) Corrupt Democrat leaders put America last.

2572) Your life matters.
2573) Your property matters.
2574) Your dollar matters.
2575) Your safety matters.

2576) Democrat invasions matter and need to be stopped.
2577) Promote jobs not mobs or society becomes a slob.

2578) Muslims are not an ethnicity – they are a belief.
2579) Muslims choose to reject revealed resurrection for Islam.

2580) Gratefulness does not exist without God's grace.

2581) I am not the tree beside me.
2582) I am not the places I have lived.
2583) I am not the places I have worked.
2584) I am the spiritual state of heart that I am in.

2585) My body is a prisoner to Earth for now.
2586) My soul has the key to Heaven.
2587) My body will rise from Earth's dust in Christ's rapture.

2588) Using invaders to pretend Democrat's value human's aborts reality.
2589) Expect political leaders to like truth and reality.
2590) Expect political leaders to govern with truth and reality.

2591) I seek out truth versus lies; Christ's Bible gives guidance.
2592) I hunt truth like children hunt Easter eggs one at a time.
2593) When I started hunting truth nuggets - I figured I might find a lot.
2594) One does not need to be a genius to hunt for truth.
2595) One does not need to be a genius to hunt for Easter eggs.

2596) Vote for holy laws and against demonic laws.
2597) Demons exist where people exist.
2598) Demonic laws do not guide the Republican Party.
2599) Demonic laws are used by the Democrat Party.
2600) Lies are Demonic activity and Democrats put them into law.

SECTION 14:

2601) The Super Ghost over all ghosts = Christ's Holy Ghost.
2602) Christ's Holy Ghost defeated all death Demons bring.
2603) Christ's Holy Ghost is over good Angels.
2604) Christ's Holy Ghost is the Ghost of eternal life.
2605) Christ's Holy Ghost is the Ghost of true hope.
2607) Christ's Holy Ghost is the Ghost of true comfort.
2608) Christ's Holy Ghost surrounds everyone.
2609) Christ's Holy Ghost indwells Christian's souls.
2610) Christ's Holy Ghost is whom Christians can pray with.
2611) Christ's Holy Ghost is whom Christians can walk with.
2612) Christ's Holy Ghost communes with repentant Christians.
2613) Christ's Holy Ghost convicts unrepentant Christians.
2614) Christ's Holy Ghost gives Spiritual fruit in Christians.
2615) Christ's Holy Ghost is very undervalued today.
2616) Christ's Holy Ghost is not well known by many today.
2617) Christ's Holy Ghost intercedes for us in prayer.
2618) Christ's Holy Ghost intercedes for us regularly.
2619) Christ's Holy Ghost intercedes when we ask Him to.
2620) Christians need regular awareness of God's Spirit.
2621) Christians need to follow God's Spirit.
2622) Christians need to obey God's Spirit fruit.
2623) Communing with God's Spirit is sound mindedness.

2624) We need to regularly renew communion with God's Spirit.
2625) I am grateful for God-Christ's-Spirit.

2626) I can't count enemies, but God has count of every hair.
(Luke 12:7)

2627) Freezing rain in cold regions during Noah's flood = Ice Age.

2628) Hellophobia is a legitimate fear not phobia - for those who reject
Christ.
2629) If someone still rejects Christ - they need more fear of Hell.
2630) A believer in Christ does not need to be afraid of Hell.

2631) He who flushes his toilet is likely a favorable mate.

2632) Nothing matters if the Son of God does not matter.

2633) Love people Christ's way.

2634) Know your value from Christ's cross view.

2635) I want to figure it out and my God has the answers.

2636) Churches simply need to screw their head on tightly.

2637) Don't try to set evil records - they all get destroyed.

2638) There are good nerve vibes not just bad ones.
2639) I don't believe in role models.
2640) The Holy Spirit is my guide.
2641) I am not Christ.
2642) I cannot be like Christ.
2643) I can follow Christ.
2644) I can walk with His Holy Spirit.
2645) I can deny myself like Christ some.
2646) Christ's Spirit is nearest to being my role model.
2647) Christ's Spirit fruit is something I enjoy.
2648) Christ's Spirit fruit is something I follow.
2649) I can't know everything like Christ.
2650) I have to deal with my knowledge level.
2651) My knowledge level + Christ's Holy Spirit.
2652) My knowledge level + Intercession.
2653) My knowledge level + Christ's words.

2654) Discriminate like a tree.
2655) Stay rooted in Christ's wells of life.

2656) Common sins are mismanagement of basic appetites.

2657) Truth reassures confidence in proper direction.

2658) There is a thin line between buzz and drunk.
2659) Be wise and be filled with Christ's Spirit.
2660) Be wise and choose Christ's Spirit over medicine.
2660) Be wise and don't underestimate the risks of medicine.
2661) Be wise and only use minimal doses of medicine.
2662) Be wise and favor abstinence.
2663) Be wise and study nutrition.
2664) Be wise and know medicine is in caffeine drinks.
2665) Be wise and repent from gluttony.
2666) There is more variation in bullying & lies than progressive jazz.
2667) Don't blame everything on medicine.
2668) Rebuke bullies, swindlers and thieves in society.
2669) Put swindler group's medicines into Doctors hands.
2670) Swindler medicines can be weakened like any other.
2671) True Justice loves God and neighbors.

2672) We aren't superman but can trust proven supernatural plans.

2673) Safety can be boring, but it is good.
2674) Reckless stunts are unnecessary risks.
2675) People dealings have necessary and unnecessary risk.
2676) Heroes sometimes do unsafe things.
2677) Selecting and making new acquaintances can be a risk.
2678) Be discerning for safety but life has risks.

2679) Trust God's axis just like the Earth.

2680) Politicians have been major thieves via Science.
2681) Democrat politicians falsify many Sciences.
2682) Democrats declare people should not have cars.
2683) Democrats demonize medicine for cartels sake.

2684) There is righteous justification in every truth.
2685) There is a misleading deceptive trick in every lie.

2686) Faith expects rain when a weatherman says 99% chance.
2687) Faith expects eternal life in the 100% resurrected Christ.
2688) Grace does not give reign to destroyers.
2689) Grace gives salvation from destruction.
2690) Grace does not come from the enemy of God's 10 commands.

2691) When grace is not exercised - God has been ignored.

2692) "Big Foot" myths don't intrigue me - Gorilla's exist in reality.

2693) People need a heart lift not a face lift.

2694) In God's eyes - Abortionists are murderers.

2695) Words matter = We are a word created by the Word.
(John 1)

2696) Real fast food = An apple. Get it? A fruit fasting food.

2697) God forgives and saves repentant baby killers.

2698) Prosperity is not prosperity unless used for Heaven.

2699) Our own mind is more threatening to us than Satan.

2700) If mercy is not put into action it just looks like a word on paper.

2701) An overly judgmental person doesn't want to know anyone.
2702) Ecclesiastes regularly steers my mind = "Life is short".

2703) Faith is necessary because none of us know very much.

2704) If Christ is not your light on Earth - He won't be in the next life.

2705) Wake up to infinite reality.

2706 I do not oppose a LITTLE humor.

2707) There is no grace without supreme love.

2708) Scientists lie - carbon dating has a shelf life.

2709) The best thing a parent guardian can do is share Christ.

2710) Without forgiveness nobody lives.

2711) The concept of forgiveness could not have come from man.

2712) Forgiveness is supernatural evidence of God's superior wisdom.

2713) Everybody dies - Christ rose from the dead.

2714) Christ turned the symbolic tree of death into a life producing tree.

2715) Pure freedom gives regard for life not disregard.

2716) The value of grace and truth repetition is revealed each morning.

2717) There is a thin line between pride and shame - have mercy.

2718) Nothing God says is extreme.
2719) What God says is just, merciful, and lovely.
2720) Those who oppose God's order are extremists.

2721) Honor Christ's eternal gravity.

2722) God restored Samson before he died.

2723) Unite with life, divide with Christ.

2724) What God thinks matters.
2725) Purpose to not be concerned with people's unmerciful views.

2726) Christ is Lord of all Seasons.

2727) If you love destruction, destroy your future in Hell.
2728) Believe in Christ's love, redemption and eternal joy.

2729) Sunrise symbolizes Christ's resurrection.
2730) Sunset symbolizes the coming of death.
2731) It is unfortunate that people see daily restoration evidence and reject Christ.

2732) God gives us water under our tongue in saliva glands.

2733) People disappoint but God appoints us to extend kindness.

2734) Today is the best day to trust God's eternal peace.

2735) Noah's Ark was God's lifeboat.

2736) Christ did not die for $1 trillion; He died for dying souls.

2737) Bless Heaven and Earth with more Godly love, trust Christ.

2738) Love God, care for your body, enjoy life, love all, handle gently.

2739) Do not deny Christ's clues.

2740) Discriminate against slavery and for individual stewardship.

2741) Supremely wealthy = Destination Heaven = Christ's house.

2742) Absolute brilliance = The Creator of Earth.

2743) Christ is supremely diverse enough to save every willing human in History.

2744) Wisdom always supports reverence for God in politics.

2745) Everlasting faith + everlasting hope is in Christ.

2746) Christ spells love in an infinite number of ways.

2747) Christ's Heaven is too good to not be true; it is extended life.

2748) God-Christ's-Spirit has loved everyone in every generation.

2749) Evil is burdensome.

2750) God compliments us with sunshine every day.

2751) There is no investment better than a permanent investment.

2752) In truth, there is no such thing as "always an addict".

2753) God has all the answers; a humble heart receives many.

2754) Why is high IQ necessary to share Christ with billions? It isn't.

2755) Christ did not say one would have faith as big as a mustard seed.

2756) Bible Paul was basically a terrorist before converting to Christianity.

2757) Fake Scientists use to call the Bible Ancient.
2757) Fake Scientists use to talk about Science from millions of years ago.
2758) If pre-creation Science assertion were real it would be truly "ancient".
2759) Bible haters make "ancient" a negative word in reference to Bible.
2760) Bible haters make "ancient" a positive word in various false Science theory references.

2761) The Bible is not very old, but is much older than telescopes.

2762) People grow older but do not need to grow bitter.

2763) Significant perception = God generally wakes us from sleep.

2764) People purifying their hearts is the step to a better society.

2765) American Indians got to America via ships.

2766) The path of success is reverence for God.

2767) 1 husband x 1 wife producing child = 3 of a kind = family.

2768) Boats and ships existed a long time ago, Noah's Ark is evidence.

2769) If Noah could ride a ship then so could American Indians.

2770) I still say, "American Indians got to America via ships."

2780) God's love gives Winter, Spring, Summer and Autumn flavors.

2781) Sensuality worships the creation more than the Creator.

2782) Wisdom is not about money.
2783) Remember Joseph was sold by his brothers into slavery?
2784) Joseph spent 13 years in prison on a false charge.
2785) Joseph later became the wealth manager during famine.
2786) Joseph kept faith in God through his hard times.

(Genesis 39)

2787) No sacrifice is worthy of God's redemption, except Jesus.

2788) Obvious sense needs to become more common.

2789) Life comes from its virgin born power source.

2790) Evolution was the leading vehicle of racism last century.

2791) Democrats led racism via slavery, KKK, Evolution & false accusations.
2792) Democrats lead racism via reverse psychology with false racism claims.
2793) Democrats also lead racism via conspired drug cartel schemes.
2794) Democrats also lead racism via Islamic cult promotions.
2795) Democrats also lead racism via lying about stats for delusional, divisive revenge.
2796) Democrats also lead racism by ignoring the outlawing of slavery.

2797) The heart is easier to teach than the mind.
2798) Forgiveness ushers the King of teachers for hearts.
2799) God's Spirit fruit teaches the heart.
2800) God's Spirit fruit convicts the heart.

SECTION 15:

2801) There is no better choice than the Creator of day.

2802) Explore God's artistry in the fruit of the Spirit.

2803) Be an infinite child for life, not destruction.

2804) We can enjoy music forever in Christ.

2805) With Christ as Lord we are an "Infinite Child".

2806) Merciless Hell already exists inside many people.

2807) We still know very little of God's scope.

2808) Humans have not even come close to thinking everything.

2809) There is plenty of room for original thought creations.

2810) There are words beyond words to discuss in Heaven's future.

2811) Evolution cannot choose but creation can.

2812) We cannot evolve anything; we create like our Creator, but limited.

2813) God is equally against racist Black Panther and KKK groups.

2814) Eternal sharing is faiths higher learning degree in Christ.

2815) A fictional Christ who supports abortion is worthless to pro-eternal life.

2816) Christ came to fulfill "thou shalt not kill" not throw the law out.

2817) Christ adds value, and understanding to the law.

2818) Christ gives temporary and eternal mercy with the law.

2819) Christ's eternal mercy is for eternally transfigured believers.

2820) We will no longer sin in Heaven; earthly mercy is celebrated.

2821) Lasting beauty is in the heart of eternal peace.

2822) Natural Fatherhood matters.

2823) Death is stronger than me but not stronger than Christ.

2824) I believe I am related to Samson not evolution.

2825) Balance moral rights and stewardship boundaries.

2826) One who will lie about Heaven will lie about anything.

2827) Good luck increases when you cater to its potential.

2828) "Thou shalt not steal" even protects the thief.

2829) Over punishing a repentant thief is also stealing.
2830) People stalemate redemption by speculating repentance.
2831) Speculating repentance pessimistically is not proper.
2832) Teach repentance and have clear achievement measures.
2833) Don't obstruct reconciliation with doubt, fear and negativity.
2834) Do not be a tempter, negative seed planter, Devil's advocate.
2835) Repentance reveals a spirit of awareness and good works.
2836) Repentance does not mean perfection or temptation immunity.
2837) Repentance does not mean a person won't fall again.
2838) Repentance is a reset of heart & mind with desire of the new path.
2839) Repentance inspires a person to exercise a good conscience.
2840) Hi-jacking a repentant walk is wrong; our capability measures tasks.
2841) The repentant in reconciliation settings fulfill duties and pay debts.
2842) The repentant person is always learning.
2843) Christ's Spirit is the only perfect teacher, thus we promote liberty.
2844) Who can the repentant rationally learn from 24/7 except Christ?
2845) All have sinned do not obstruct physical redemption with doubt.
2846) Do not obstruct physical redemption with nitpicking.
2847) Do not obstruct physical redemption with spite.
2848) Do not obstruct physical redemption with temptation tests.
2849) Do not obstruct physical redemption by raising the standard.
2850) Let a person pay their debt, follow peacemaking standards & let
them become free from deficit.
2851) Instill Christ's ways when in a system.
2852) Promote Christ's teaching where people resolve things on their
own.
2853) All hearts and minds always need conscientiousness practice.

2854) Christ's "Golden Rule" clearly applies in numerous situations.

2855) Reconciliation measures are easy, except many don't cooperate.
2856) People who don't cooperate in systems are not peacemaking.
2857) Not peacemaking in a system won't peace make elsewhere.
2858) People have disagreements; there are peaceable ways to disagree.
2859) Discerning when it is safe to release an offender is not so easy.
2860) Courts give sentencing times, but cautionary signs should reassess.
2861) The safety of the general public is important.
2862) Violent Prisoners should prove peaceable before being released.

2863) A person in detainment has time to prove they can be peaceable.
2864) Why is a prisoner angry at others if he or she does show consistent
peace attempts?

2865) Don't be too nitpicky, but people should show peacemaking effort.
2866) Reconciliation systems should expect consistent peacemaking habits.

2867) The word "peacemaking" is not used enough.
2868) Cultures think it right to show they can defend themselves.
2869) A defense shield without a peacemaking sign appears as a weapon.
2870) People have to learn that peacemaking talks and stances are required.
2871) People can talk defense, but peacemaking diplomacy is standard.
2872) The standard is not clear today, but should clearly be diplomacy.
2873) Diplomacy and peacemaking expect patience.
2874) Diplomacy and peacemaking expect time to think.
2875) Diplomacy and peacemaking set aside pride. (lying isn't peace)
2876) People who won't set pride aside aren't interested in peacemaking.
2877) People with pride may have a form of peace via forced pacifism.
2878) People with pride may be peaceable with some as their respected bully.
2879) Bullies do not maintain peace and liberty - they control people.
2880) Bullies control habits result in impulsiveness.
2881) Many think bullying works to keep teams working together.
2882) Bullying can work similar to having a head manager, but without ethics.
2883) Legitimate management has ethics, bullying lacks ethics.
2884) Managers are equally under law, bullies seek immunity.
2885) Bullies break laws and set up others to take their fall.
2886) Bullies create immunity and increase in greed.
2887) Bullies vary: Some bullies love violence, power or convenience.
2888) 'Convenience' loving bullies are manipulators and swindlers.
2889) Greed leading to violence also occurs with a 'convenience bully'.

2890) All prison standards should rise expecting peacemaking & diplomacy.
2891) Prisoners should be expected to exercise diplomacy & peacemaking.
2892) Prisoners should be expected to show dignity among peers.
2893) Prisoners should be expected to adopt peacemaking ethics.
2894) Prisoners should be expected to adopt diplomacy ethics.
2895) Prisoners should be expected to have a dignified culture.

2896) Prisoners may argue against diplomacy, but make it a written rule.
2897) Shelters should have the Prison rules of peacemaking & diplomacy.

2898) Halfway houses should have peacemaking & diplomacy rules.
2899) Shelters should have peacemaking & diplomacy written down.
2900) Halfway houses should have peacemaking & diplomacy written down.

2901) Sharing Christ is the ultimate good job all are commanded to do.
2902) Sharing Christ believes in Christ as Lord and people as neighbors.
2903) Sharing Christ is not always in words, some are not good orators.
2904) Sharing Christ is being a peacemaker.
2905) Sharing Christ is following His ten commandments.
2906) Sharing Christ is ultimately forgiving and choosing diplomacy.
2907) Sharing Christ is walking in forgiveness with the Spirit.
2908) Sharing Christ is the fruit of the Spirit.
2909) The fruit of the Spirit is in Galatians 5 - love, joy, peace...
2910) Sharing Christ is seeking truth over lies.
2911) Sharing Christ is many things, but starts with faith in Christ.
2912) Sharing Christ compels unbelievers who recognize peace is right.
2913) Sharing Christ compels unbelievers for survival morals.
2914) Christ commandments being known are how society survives; His commandments being revered is how society has good successes.
2915) Society does not survive without "thou shalt not kill".
2916) Society does not survive without "thou shalt not steal".
2917) Society does not survive without God's ten commandments.
2918) God-Christ's-Spirit teaches us to be calm.
2919) Jesus taught repenting of anger to avoid violence.
(Matthew 5:22)

2920) Repenting of anger detours violence.
2921) Jesus demands we repent of anger.
2922) Jesus cites danger of Hell for simply being angry.
2923) Jesus cites danger of Hell for using insults while angry.
2924) Jesus cites danger of Hell equally for murder & unrepentant anger.

2925) Living in unrepentant anger is rejecting God's Spirit of Peace.

2926) Resurrected God = Power of life Religion
2927) Resurrected God = Living Religion.
2928) Resurrected God = True Religion.
2929) Resurrected God = Proven Religion.
2930) Resurrected God = Loving Religion.
2931) Resurrected God = Forgiving Religion.
2932) Resurrected God = Heavenly Religion.
2933) Resurrected God = 2nd life Religion

2934) Resurrected God = Infinite Religion.
2935) Resurrected God = Comforting Religion.
2936) Resurrected God = Religion of true hope.
2937) Resurrected God = Religion of lasting hope.
2938) Resurrected God = Religion of eternal Truth.
2939) Resurrected God = Religion of Good Spirit.
2940) Resurrected God = Religion of joy.
2941) Resurrected God = Religion of goodness.
2942) Resurrected God = Religion of eternal peace.

2943) Salvation does not come from unforgiveness.
2944) Salvation does not come from mercilessness or powerlessness.
2945) Salvation does not come from dead gods or false gods.
2946) Salvation does not come from a cross it comes from Christ.

2947) Humility acts forgivingly, mercifully, and gracefully.

2948) People relations matter as part of "love your neighbor".

2949) Do not die in eternal ignorance.

2950) Slave to Satan or child of God-Christ's-Spirit?

2951) Real people are sinners and they know it.

2952) A fake person thinks they have never done any wrong.

2953) Godly encouragement and truth do more than money.
2954) Pursue humble God awareness in every setting.

2955) Christ is good reason for everyone to pursue good.
2956) Christ is good reason for any believer to speak freely of Heaven.
2957) Christ is good reason for the outcast believer to speak of Heaven.
2958) Christ is good reason for any imperfect believer to share gospel.

2959) Christ is more than a name and Savior, He is the Spirit fruit.
2960) Christ is more than a name and Savior, He is life versus death.
2961) Christ is more than a name and Savior, He is the Commandments.
2962) Christ is more than a name and Savior, He is the forgiver.
2963) Christ is more than a name and Savior, He casts people into Hell.
2964) Christ is more than a name and Savior, He lets people in Heaven.

2965) Life is often an observation of human error and the hero.

2966) Rise with Christ the Hero, not with your own ceiling.

2967) Basic success is not boast of vainly – it's true peace in your heart.
2968) The false evolutionary theory is racism's mind revealed.

2969) Give generations of children their real parents with natural marriage laws.

2970) God is more beautiful than all characters.
2971) God is more beautiful than the seashores.
2972) God is more beautiful than our best laughs.
2973) God is beautiful because He created character, seas and joys.
2974) Christ's redemption is beautiful far beyond slow jazz music.
2975) Christ's redemption includes the seashores.
2976) Christ's redemption includes laughter and joy.
2977) Christ's redemption includes the personalities He created.
2978) Christ's redemption includes music in Heaven.
2979) Christ's redemption is a preeminent beautiful peace.

2980) Do not be afraid of peace for fear of losing it, trust Christ.

2981) Christ paid the price of death to show His resurrection life path.

2982) Connect all the dots of the Bible to Christ.
2983) Set aside what you don't understand for later.
2984) Pray about what does not make sense.
2985) Rules were strict in the Old Testament, but forgiveness existed.
2986) God provided the sacrifice lamb offerings for repentance.
2987) Medicines did not exist in the Old Testament like today.
2988) Without medicine strict living rules were needed to prevent disease.
2989) I don't know the reasons for strict rules, but clearly there was reason.
2990) I gave examples of logical reasons for strict rules = preventing disease.
2991) Connect the dots of forgiveness complimenting peace.
2992) Connect the dots of supreme forgiveness coming from Christ.
2993) Connect the dots of forgiveness complimenting wisdom.
2994) Connect the dots of forgiveness getting rid of stress.
2995) Connect the dots of peace complimenting joy.
2996) Connect the dots of temperance complimenting patience.
2997) Connect the dots of temperance coming from God's Holy Spirit.
2998) Connect the dots of temperance helping physical coordination.

2999) Connect the dots of temperance helping orderly planning.
3000) Connect the dots of temperance valuing peripheral awareness.
3001) Connect all the dots to Christ's forgiveness and resurrection.
3002) Connect the dots of resurrection and redemption.
3003) Connect the dots of redemption every morning.
3004) Connect the dots that redeeming liberty works in business.
3005) Connect the dots that people need liberty for oxygen.
3006) Connect the dots that people need regular redemption.
3007) Connect the dots that people redeem with Christ on their own.
3008) Connect the dots that Christ redeems you not someone else.
3009) Connect that your paid debts should redeem you to people.
3010) Connect that you redeem yourself with Christ on your own errors.
3011) Connect that we have liberty to work out things with Christ.
3012) Connect that we don't need people for most errors, but Christ.
3013) Connect that a few USA founders understood liberty in Christ.
3014) Connect that some are spoiled by using liberty for greed.
3015) Connect that many are grateful for liberty and revere God.
3016) Connect that some self-righteous want to take people's liberty.
3017) Connect that some think their preference is law and judge wrongly.
3018) Connect a whole lot of things, and refer to Christ's forgiveness.
3019) Connect a lot of things and refer to Christ's redemption.
3020) Connect a lot of things and refer to a peacemaking standard.
3021) Connect a lot of things and value truth over lies.

3022) Value truth over lies particularly in theology and politics.
3023) Value truth over lies period, but honest laws affect everyone.
3024) Value truth over lies period, but honest laws affect minds.
3025) Value truth in theology because it affects the heart, soul & mind.
3026) Lies over truth are often for petty theft by a thief or swindler.
3027) Lies over truth are often for a manipulating micro manager.
3028) Lies over truth are often for a control freak.
3029) Lies for control freaks are sin also, and destructive.
3030) Lies in politics and theology destroy nations foundationally.

3031) Highly value knowing the truth in theology and politics.
3032) Highly value teachers of truth in theology and politics.
3033) Highly value sharing truth teachings in theology and politics.
3034) Highly value supporting truth in theology and politics.
3035) Highly value teaching truth in theology and politics.
3036) Highly value loving God & neighbors with theology and politics.

3037) Godly justice reveres God and our neighbor's well-being.

3038) Positive reality = Jesus saves until the end of the World.
3039) Negative reality = We can die any day.

1 John 4:8 "He that loves not knows not God for God is love."

John 10:9 "If you will confess with your mouth that Jesus Christ is Lord and believe in your heart that God has raised Him from the dead, you will be saved."

1 Timothy 2:4 "God wants all people to be saved, and to come to the knowledge of the truth."

CONCLUSION:

1) Clean your heart and mind daily.
2) Pray, "Lord correct my spiritual and mental vision."
3) Check your own motives regularly.
4) Repent of vain motives regularly.
5) Have confidence in Christ's forgiveness.
6) Know Christ wants you being fruitful.
7) Know Christ redeems because He loves us.
8) Know Christ redeems us to be fruitful.
9) Know Christ's redemption matters - not oppressors.
10) Forgive and work around silencing oppressors.
11) Be patient and learn what you can where you are.
12) "Being fruitful" covers everything:
13) "Being fruitful" is learning, sharing, praying, repenting...
14) God encourages fruitfulness with Heavenly rewards.
15) Be urgent because Hell is real and life is short.
16) Be hopeful in wanting people to choose Heaven.
17) Be eager to give thorough clarity for eternal choice.
18) Be eager to give thorough clarity for trusting Christ.
19) Politics matter for the freedom to share.
20) Politics matter for the freedom to have private property.
21) Politics matter for insisting we want authorities under God.
22) Politics matter if you want freedom to read the Bible.
23) Support politics that allow you to read the Bible.
24) Support politics that allow you to compare the Bible.
25) Support politics that allow evidence of true vs. false gods.
26) Support politics that don't silence truth about false religions.
27) Support peace, repentance and redemption "under God".

GOD IS LOVE POEM

A beach with a palm tree,
The sky full of doves,
Not half as beautiful as is God's love.

Higher than the mountains,
Deeper than the seas,
Love so benevolent,
To meet your deepest need.

Reality Harmonizer Bob

References: Christ's Bible, Wikipedia, Politico Fact, "Planet MySkull".

"Planet MySkull" is my name for the brain within my skull.

Reality Harmonizer Bob

www.ingramcontent.com/pod-product-compliance
Lightning Source LLC
Chambersburg PA
CBHW081416250726
48654CB00013B/1717